Sabine Huschka, Barbara Gronau (eds.)
Energy and Forces as Aesthetic Interventions

Theatre Studies | Volume 123

SABINE HUSCHKA, BARBARA GRONAU (EDS.)

Energy and Forces as Aesthetic Interventions

Politics of Bodily Scenarios

[transcript]

The publication is a result of the DFG research project ›Transgressionen‹, which is based at HZT – Inter-University Centre for Dance Berlin and Berlin University of Arts (UdK) – funded by the German Research Foundation.

Gefördert durch

Bibliographic information published by the Deutsche Nationalbibliothek
The Deutsche Nationalbibliothek lists this publication in the Deutsche Nationalbibliografie; detailed bibliographic data are available in the Internet at http://dnb.d-nb.de

Cover layout: Maria Arndt, Bielefeld
Cover illustration: Frontcover: »Ah! Oh! A Contemporary Ritual«, choreographed by Kat Válastur, photographed by Dorothea Tuch. Backcover: »Blind Spotting Performance Series«, choreographed by Margrét Sara Guðjónsdóttir, photographed by David Kiers.
Proofread by Ali Jones and Malte Pieper
Typeset by Francisco Bragança, Bielefeld
Printed by Majuskel Medienproduktion GmbH, Wetzlar
Print-ISBN 978-3-8376-4703-7
PDF-ISBN 978-3-8394-4703-1
https://doi.org/10.14361/9783839447031

Table of Contents

Energy and Forces as Aesthetic Interventions
An Introduction

Sabine Huschka and Barbara Gronau

> In the meantime, I am talking less about states than about energies. Does something have its own energy and, if so, how do I get access to it? How can we channel energy and bring it into a form? The body is not a piano! (Meg Stuart 2018)

The recourse to the energetic in the performing arts appears in various constellations and has become increasingly differentiated in recent decades. Whether in theatre, dance or performance art, within the concept of energy and its expression in forces, the immaterial and medial conditions of artistic representation are always accompanied by the attempt to grasp their effects. Talking about energy means considering a key cultural term that reveals decisive upheavals in people's understandings. Especially in contemporary theatre, energetic processes form the very centre of artistic practice, and they pervade dance, performance art and theatre: Bodies and constellations are transformed through them, specific states and forces are evoked, and intensive or even collective effects are produced. It can be observed that, since the beginning of modernity, energetic states acquired their own aesthetic relevance and meaning. The energetic is now no longer the mere condition of forms, but rather maintains the function of aesthetic interventions themselves.

This volume investigates the aesthetic potential of the energetic. It explores the contemporary, historical, aesthetic and praxeological approaches to ›energy‹ by discussing concepts of this dazzling figure of thought and discourse, which itself considers the energetic between overwhelming experience, cosmic grounding, and transformational force. Their consequent observations and analyses raise central questions, such as: what exactly is revealed by the energetic as an aesthetic potential? What transgressive potential can an artistic work unfurl upon forces?

When energy is defined as »force, energy [*Tatkraft*], efficiency, as well as force of character, insistence, [... and as] the capability to do work« at the beginning of the 20th century (Meyer's great encyclopedia of conversations 1908: 774), two concepts can be recognized: the ancient *dynamis* on the one hand, and the concept of force developed by Newtonian physics on the other. In addition to their capability of shaping, force describes each of the nature's changes in state and interactions, the intensity of which is measurable. They thus refer to a generative dimension of nature – which, as used in reference to willpower here – will also be extended to cultural and social constellations. Under the influence of thermodynamics and the theory of relativity, the concept of energy in modernity was transformed into a purely abstract variable of state, even though its numerous concrete manifestations remain perceptible and measurable.

The realization that these diverse forms of energy could be converted led the philosopher Fritz Mauthner to the realization that there is »more unity than could be previously fathomed in world events« (Mauthner 1923: 409). As a result, energy is now considered to be a universal quantity, alongside space and time, in the natural sciences. When discussing concepts of energy and power in the arts, the principles of form and performance, as well as those of interaction and transgression, appear to be of more particular importance than others.

As the energetic has rarely been developed as an aesthetic category in dance and theatre studies, it lacks any analytical and theoretical transparency about which scholars could come to a mutual understanding. This volume therefore proposes new discursive approaches, with which it will become possible to analyze performances, scenic performances, or dance techniques as aesthetic structures, based upon their energetic qualities and figurations. Of particular interest to this inquiry are those practices that convert the body's gift of moving itself into an aesthetic work containing energies and forces, following the intense desire for transgression, intensification and transformation. The contributions included in this volume thus explore not only real strategies but also the utopian possibilities of such aesthetic interventions, which oscillate between critique and longing for transgression and harmony, respectively.

When energetic processes in dance and performance art are qualified as the mobilization, activation, initiation, regulation, guidance and containment of forces, what consequently follows is that not only aesthetic, but also ecological, economic and political relations come up for debate. On the one hand, this concerns the ways in which the energetic becomes perceivable via staged, experimental or choreographic arrangements. On the other hand, this also concerns the interactive relations of exchange between subjects and objects. Moreover, within every execution of movement reside political and economic corporeal ideas of power and exhaustion, of form and transgression, and of giving and taking. The energetic – as the contributions in this volume demonstrate – is therefore the main focus of debate in the performing arts even above all other politics of perception and corporeality.

The collected contributions presented here originate from the artistic-academic symposium »*Energetic Forces as Aesthetic Interventions*«, which was held in June 2018 at the Inter-University Center for Dance (Hochschulübergreifendes Zentrum Tanz, HZT) in Berlin, and was attended by international scholars and artists. The symposium was organized in cooperation with the DFG research project *Transgressions: Energization of Bodies and Scenes*, which was conducted in cooperation with the *Faculty of Performing Arts of Berlin University of the Arts (Fakultät Darstellende Kunst der Universität der Künste Berlin)*. The symposium offered the chance for dance and theatre scholars, alongside choreographers Kat Válastur and Margrét Sara Guðjónsdóttir, to engage in intensive discussions regarding how energetic processes can transform into aesthetic forces, and which potentiality can be attributed to these aesthetic interventions.

This productive, shared space for thinking was located between praxeological, aesthetic and discourse-analytical perspectives, and it demonstrated the inherent connections of historical and contemporary approaches and conceptions of the energetic, alongside the body-political questions that became apparent during the symposium's lectures, lecture demonstrations and workshops. As one physical reverberation of the symposium, this volume therefore presents two artist's statements and interviews, in addition to scholarly contributions from the fields of dance, theatre and cultural studies. The wide horizon of positions and discussion formats assembled in this volume encompass questions of which functions and promises might go hand in hand with the energetic as an aesthetic force field, as well as how these energizations can be described and analyzed in dance and performance.

This volume thus advocates a necessary strengthening of discourse in dance studies, as well as approaches to the interdisciplinary exchange with theatre studies, in which a resonating space between theoretical and practical forms of knowledge might be achieved. The nationally and internationally renowned academic voices assembled here therefore claim a politically relevant field of discourse regarding energy and power, while also providing a heuristic contouring of their aesthetic, analytical and historical perspective. The socio-political resonances of bodies are illuminated in various performances. Overheated, endangered and tired bodies can be found in *24 Hour Happening* (1965) with Joseph Beuys, Bazon Brock and Wolf Vostell et al., in Valie Exports' *Hyperbulie* (1973), in *10000 Gestures* (2017) by Boris Charmatz or the series *Men in the Cities* by Robert Longo. In addition, this can also be found in the interplay of body and energy in the practices of ballet and somatics, as well as in contact improvisation such as the movement-training practice of Gaga created by the Israeli choreographer Ohad Naharin. In addition, the essays in this volume also examine; Isadora Duncan, Martha Graham and Toni Bentley's historical discourses of the energetic; Rudolf von Laban's praxeological movement theories of the energetic; Randy Martin's sociological drafts of the aesthetic and mobilizing force of dance; Christoph Menke's aesthetic theories of force; and Alfred North Whitehead and Gilbert Simondon's (natural) philosophical ideas on the cosmological, particularly in the context of debates on posthumanism. This multitude of approaches is organized into the following four areas:

Practices, Discourses and Politics of the ›Energetic‹

The volume opens with a contribution by Barbara Gronau on the cultural-historical process of gaining perspective on the sites of energetic processes. In response to the question *How to Talk About Energy?* Gronau emphasizes the importance of the performing arts as a practice of production and that of making energetic processes perceptible. The contribution develops central aspects of discourses on energy within the performing arts during the 20th and 21st centuries, alongside three specific characteristics: the performers' handling of their own bodies, the search for new ways to impact and affect the audience, and the interrogation of the very concept of »artistic work«. Gronau thereby also simultaneously defines scenic realizations as epistemic constellations in which the energetic appears as a figure of knowledge generated by theatrical and discursive techniques. By combining body concepts and economic discourses, Gronau simultaneously emphasizes the necessity of a transdisciplinary location for the concept of energy. Finally, in contrast to the entropy model, the balancing or transgression of forces in performances can be read as actual work on energetic states.

In her contribution *Dancing the Energy/Energizing the Dancing*, SUSAN LEIGH FOSTER examines the interdependent interplay of body and energy within various dance practices. The analytical question of *how energy is conceptualized* focuses on movement techniques and practices in ballet, somatics, and contact improvisation as examples of embodied theories of physical energies and their subsequent operations. How energy is addressed verbally or physically, which interactions between the dancing bodies are promoted or inhibited, and which aesthetic ideals materialize through energetic processes, are all manifested through different policies of perception. These, interestingly enough, manifest themselves as generally variable body politics connected to the physical labor that is an integral part of dancing: the aim is either to aesthetically render the invisibility of power, or to make the power and energy that is nevertheless always physically demanded visible. At the same time, Foster reveals analogies between contemporary forms of training that – regardless of their stylistic aesthetic difference – are aimed at establishing an efficiency and optimization strategy of the energetic household of dancing bodies. On the basis of an incorporated anatomical-biomechanical knowledge and imagination-supported procedures, increasingly virtuosic and fluctuating but, at the same time economizing, approaches are applied to the energetic potential of the body, which is regarded as inexhaustible and valuable. In terms of choreographic analyses, Foster concludes that investigations of energetic processes reveal valuable aspects of the production of meaning, as their modes of production and distribution refer to the construction of physical identities in dance and its processes.

In her contribution *Aesthetic Scenarios of Energeia: Bodies as Transformational Fields of Force*, SABINE HUSCHKA interrogates contemporary choreographers' interest in applying themselves to aesthetic work with energy. Some thoroughly diverging aesthetic conceptions and interrogated discourse figurations of energy (i.e. Meg Stuart, Doris Uhlich, Boris Charmatz, Merce Cunningham and Margrét Sara Guðjónsdóttir) reveal a conspicuous desire for transgression that, in contrast to our life-worldly disposition of rampant exhaustion, deems the body to be its own unique reservoir of strength. This calls upon a transgressive, transformational and transforming potential of movement, which ignites aesthetic work on movements' initiation moments occurring at the very limits of the body. Building upon this idea, and in dialogue with scholarly perspectives on the political potential of energy (Foster, Lepecki), as well as with philosophical figures of thought regarding transgression (Foucault), Huschka notes a fundamental characteristic of the dance-aesthetic work on *energeia*: namely indicating the creation of aesthetic fields of transgression, which allow one to conceive of the body as a utopian instance. Movement scenarios of *energeia* thus pass the political potential for action over to the body.

In a discourse-analytical investigation of female dancers' autobiographies, CHRISTINA THURNER unfolds the way in which the energetic as an aesthetic figuration of dance gains significance. Beginning with Isadora Duncan's modern concept of offering the dancing body as an aesthetic form grounded in an »original source of all movement«, Thurner examines historically determinative discourse figurations. As formulated experiences, narratives and phenomena, these establish a dynamic discursive field of the energetic. Methodologically, Thurner strives for a critical reading of the genre of autobiography, which has so far been only uncritically addressed as source material in scholarly research. Relying on Isadora Duncan's *Memoirs (Memoiren)*, Toni Bentley's *Dancer's Journal*, and Martha Graham's *Blood Memory*, she works out three formative aesthetic figurations of the energetic. (1) Graham and Duncan focus on specific scenes of the *activation and mobilization* of forces, which emerge in various ways from the relationship between the body and the world. As a result, two different configurations of the interplay of energy and body become recognizable, which can, in some instances, be understood as a vitalistic principle (Graham), while at other times it can be interpreted as the physical reverberation of a perception translated into movement (Duncan). (2) As an aesthetic scene, the energetic also calls for processes of *regulating and directing forces*. As Thurner makes clear, these correspond to a final figuration: (3) namely the reflection of perceptions of *physical ener-*

gy consumption traversed by *real experiences of exhaustion.* Striking differences in modern aesthetic concepts can be identified here. While Duncan understands the spectrum of sensations bundled within her as a continuous transposition of the energetic, and thus designs her own dancing entropically, Graham and Bentley are confronted with the impending exhaustion of their own forces, which construes the energetic of their dancing as a fire now flickering and dying.

The ›Energetic‹ as Aesthetic: Philosophical Approaches

Two contributions in this volume present concise theoretical frames that address the aesthetic obstinacy of the energetic and interrogate its philosophical figurations. Against the background of a differentiation of *Energetic Forces as Aesthetic Forces,* GERALD SIEGMUND works out the anthropologically divided nature of energetic forces. Their aesthetic power shows itself in an always already-given double movement, i.e. by constantly undoing what they simultaneously produce. Energetic forces blatantly refer to the understanding of man as a divided being, which Michel Foucault described as the historical doubling of man upon his entry into modernity: from then on, the thinking of him and of himself moves in a split sphere, which opens a space for not-knowing within knowledge itself. According to Siegmund, in light of this phenomenological »ontology of the un-thought«, dance opens up precisely this dimension of aesthetic-thinking, which allows us to rediscover another side of existence. This includes: forces, pulsations and energies that, being outside our cognitive selves, allow us to discover something that we could not yet have conceived of on our own.

Siegmund thus points to an aesthetic dimension of energetic forces, to which he attributes special qualities: energy mobilizes, activates and regulates the body, and simultaneously integrates it into a process in which energy is formed, connected, separated and released. Through his engagement with the American dance scholar Randy Martin, Siegmund expands Martin's understanding of dance, according to which dance lends itself to a mobilizing force that is socially and politically effective. Siegmund confronts Martin's work with the aesthetic theory of the German philosopher Christoph Menke, and in so doing advocates an explicitly aesthetic dimension of the mobilizing force. Through the decay of form, the aesthetic dimension of the mobilizing force effectively crafts the aesthetic subject as something transgressive: a subject that emerges across disciplines and transcends its own practice through its duplicated double. For Siegmund, this indicates the location of the potential of dance, namely: using mobilizing forces to give space to a desire that could offer a reprieve from neo-liberal economic models. The aesthetic potential of this energetic therefore accomplishes transgressions and transformations of subjectivity and knowledge.

In addition to an anthropological aesthetic, MAXIMILIAN HAAS argues alongside Alfred North Whitehead and Gilbert Simondon for a natural-philosophically informed *Cosmology of Forces*, which provides an understanding of theater as a set of *Performative Fields*. In light of recent dance and performance productions that programmatically stage non-human actors – including machines, algorithms, animals, plants, or simply mere objects – Haas subjects the networked ensembles of bodies, media, and objects to a philosophical perspective, which itself reveals their peculiar ecology of events, processes, and practices to be an aesthetic-cosmological force field of particular quality. Haas does not regard their aesthetic power as a performative event generated by bodies and performers and then made effective in the theatre. Rather, he thinks of it as a dynamic force field, which produces all theatrical elements and unfolds their effects. A cosmological theory of the aesthetic is thus projected, which interprets theatre as a situational ontogenesis of its performative events; a becoming of form via distributed forces within the performative logic of the field.

If Haas understands forces as a multitude or an infinity in which they mutually define and specify each other without ever bringing the other to a standstill, then he also thereby sketches a form of aesthetic thought about performance itself. This brings relationality and processuality to the fore as the relationship between an individual and its milieu as co-constitutive and emergent as well as rooted in specific constellations of forces producing particular effects. In this way, Haas projects a cosmological order of forces, following the thought of mathematician and pragmatist philosopher Alfred North Whitehead, and French philosopher of science and technology Gilbert Simondon. While Simondon develops a historical understanding of force, originating in 19th century electrodynamics and magnetism, and transforms it into a cosmological design of ontogenetic processes, Whitehead applies the cosmological method as a mode of speculative philosophy. Haas discusses both of these theories, as well as their potential value for a conception of performativity, with which the processual emerges as a distributed interplay of forces, in addition to becoming recognizable as a conception of activity. These forces regulate relationships and are actually both constitutive of reality as well as still remaining transgressive.

Forces in Transgression

In her chapter *Gesture, Energy, Critique*, Lucia Ruprecht explores an important body-political dimension of the energetic. She emphasizes the gesture's aesthetic power of intervention as the rhythmic figuration for an interruption of the energetic. By analytically juxtaposing Robert Longo's series of images *Men in the Cities* and Boris Charmatz's group choreography *10000 Gestures (10000 Gesten)*, Ruprecht attempts to examine their repertoire of played-out gestures. She does this on the basis of a modernist understanding of the gestural, relying on the work of Bertolt Brecht and Walter Benjamin. A dialectic therefore operates within the gesture, which oscillates between kinetically stored and potential energies. Due to the gesture's capability of punctuating movement through temporarily frozen moments of posture, it has a distinct expressiveness of critical-political potential. As Ruprecht emphasizes, the gesture is accompanied by expression and reflection, with which the energetic gains aesthetic power. Ruprecht demonstrates how aesthetic figurations of the gestural can play out by analyzing Longo's monumental images. Longo's affective arrangement of tumbling bodies operates in the very face of death, and serves as a monument of energetic forces, thus allowing energetic poses to emerge. On the other hand, Charmatz's exuberant repertoire in *10000 Gestures* is dedicated to an energetic-expressive force of incessant movements, which are applied to the hectic negotiation of our over-committed bodies. An ambivalent expenditure of energy is played out here, in which the subject constantly bends to the imperative of gestural productivity and – even while feeding off of it – also throws himself out of itself. It is precisely in this situation that Ruprecht locates the critical intervention of *10000 Gestures*: in the »mastering« of the relentless creativity of neoliberal capitalism via the magic of emptying oneself right before one's eyes.

The American researcher Meghan Quinlan applies a critical cultural analysis to the popularity of Israeli choreographer Ohad Naharin's »move-

ment language« Gaga, and investigates whether it might not in fact be considered as a practice of *Training Neoliberal Dancers*. Deriving her methodology
from ethnographic research, Quinlan works out the politics of mediation in
the Gaga classes. She reveals its principles of inventing movements, of structuring improvisation, and of self-choreographing in the sense of negotiating
bodily techniques in one's own body – with reference to Randy Martin – as
a *Metatechnique*. Gaga develops a striking activation of constantly changing
energy and force fields in the body, which physically and mentally promote
and demand a willingness to transgress the boundaries of controlled mechanisms and situations, as well as the limits of one's existing movement abilities. Thematically this is a functional service of the energetic, which trains
the body via a blurring of the pedagogical norms customary to the teaching
of technique, choreography and improvisation. The body thus becomes a
malleable agent of constant transformations and – as Quinlan points out – it
is formed according to the unique economies of the neoliberal dance market,
which demand a physically, emotionally and mentally flexible, as well as especially innovative, dancer. In contrast to Gaga's explicit self-understanding,
Quinlan interprets Gaga as a technique that is not intended to provide shape
training to the dancer's body. She rather sees it as a teaching strategy of
self-formation in terms of decision-making, to which already-learned body
techniques will be transferred as regulated processes of internal negotiation.
This raises critical perspectives that reveal the inherent power structures of
the energetic, as found within strategies for activating movement forces, as
well as in manœuvres of guiding, accumulating, and economizing physical
processes.

SUSANNE FRANCO goes into great detail tracing Rudolf Laban's extensive research about analyzing the expressive-energetic quality spectrum of physical
movement. She particularly examines the extent to which energetic forces
could be colonized as an interdependency of human movements, as located
between strategies of optimization and their individual usage for free deployment. Franco's essay *Energy, Eukinetics, and Effort. Rudolf Laban's Vision
of Work and Dance* sheds light on Laban's analysis and theoretical models for
the qualification, notation and training of efficient movement sequences,
which remains fundamental even today. Franco therefore examines Laban's
systems in the context of their historical development or their culturally
contemporaneous social, philosophical and psychological theories. She also

locates them in terms of the societal perception of (physical) labor (Karl Ludwig Klages, Fritz Giese, Karl Bücher). In this way, Franco draws attention to Laban's central, differentiating phase of work on his movement theory, ultimately referred to as *Effort Theory*, which emerged during his exile in England in the 1940s due to his research on industrial movement processes. In the 1920s Laban developed several models – *choreutics* and *eukinetics* – which offer a classification of movement qualities and their dynamics (flow). In collaboration with economist Frederick Charles Lawrence, Laban later continued this work by contouring a movement training course for female workers. Franco argues that this was aimed at establishing the rhythmic principle of working movements – a thesis that challenges the basic movement analytical approach of the American Frederic W. Taylor. Laban's *Effort Theory* offers a physical way of thinking about movement as a purposefully applicable form of energetic force, in which knowledge of transformation and of one's inner intention is reflected.

Artistic Perspectives on Somatic Interventions

The volume concludes with artistic contributions from two choreographers reflecting upon their danced-somatic approaches to the energetic. They discuss this and their own movement practices, alongside personal experiences and socio-political questions. In a conversation between Icelandic choreographer MARGRÉT SARA GUÐJÓNSDÓTTIR and Sweden-based Performance Researcher SUSAN KOZEL, Guðjónsdóttir explains in detail her somatic dance practice »Full Drop into the Body«, which she developed over many years. Within the context of a completely »burnt out body's« experience of intensely physical exhaustion, Guðjónsdóttir surrendered to a conscious practice of complete surrender, which initiated a conscious listening to her own inner rhythms. This practice of non-doing opens up a unique rhythmic world of movement, which emerges as the constant and unwilling activation of one's own body. Through many years of practice, Guðjónsdóttir developed a listening access to the energetic sources of the body, letting it move, first only for herself, but eventually also for other experienced dancers. This sharing led her to apply this practice choreographically and effectively in various phases: in 2014-2015 the *Blind Spotting Performance Series* exhibited the burnt out, broken, exhausted, apathetic, imploding body in a achievement-oriented society. Strikingly set in front of red velvet theatre curtains, these performances were designed to provide as a stage for the critical antihero. Guðjónsdóttir's ongoing choreographies *Conspiracy Ceremony – HYPERSONIC STATES* (November 2017) and *Pervasive Magnetic Stimuli* (2018) continue this intensive movement research, which targets the unconscious forces that fulfill us.

In her choreographic work, the Berlin-based choreographer KAT VÁLASTUR continues this investigation in her study of *The Poetics of a Morphing Body*. In this chapter, she traces her own artistic engagement with the forces that attack, pervade and deform the body in our technological reality. She also explains her choreographic questions and their challenges to dance in great detail. For example, in *GLAND* (2014), Válastur exposed her body to a fluctuating gravitational field, constructed aesthetically with movement, which sought to interrogate the very spatiality of forces themselves. The group choreography *Ah! Oh! A Contemporary Ritual* (2014) presented a post-apocalyptic scenario. In this destructive ›landscape‹ the dancers – who are filled up with foreign forces, represented here by a tremendous quantity of data – seek to initiate ritualized force fields. They thus position themselves in space as mutating circular formations. The ongoing solo choreographed piece *Rasp Your Soul* (2017) misplaces a dancer's body in the midst of an archaic landscape. The aforementioned mutating digital data volumes have long since penetrated this body space, in order to henceforth forge a path to what is outside. This work represents a change in Válastur's choreographic perspective: it now includes the initiation of a movement-aesthetic process of the protrusion of foreign forces towards the inside, as becomes visible through a process of morphing.

Acknowledgements

We would like to thank all of the academics and artists involved for their productive collaboration, as well as for their interest and openness to the aesthetic questions of the energetic. The lively thematic debates that emerged in our conversations have been formative for this volume. Our thanks also go out to the dance scholar Susan Leigh Foster and the theatre scholar Maximilian Haas for their supplementary contributions to this book. The realization of this publication is also due in part to the committed and knowledgeable editorial work of Ali Jones. We also wish to extend our gratitude to our student assistant Malte Pieper, who tirelessly and prudently supported the DFG research project *Transgressions*, and contributed significantly to the realization of the volume. This publication is also and above all due to the financial support of the *Deutsche Forschungsgemeinschaft* (German Research Foundation). Finally, we would like to thank transcript publishing house for its unfailingly friendly, patient and capable support of us and our book project.

Works Cited

Kaminski, Astrid (2018): »Choreografin Stuart über Stuart: ›Der Körper ist kein Klavier‹. Anlass für ein Gespräch über Transformation.« *taz* (21 June 2018), www.taz.de/!5514264/ [Accessed 09 December 2018].

Meyers großes Konversations-Lexikon (1908): 6th edition, 5 volumes, (Leipzig und Wien: Bibliographisches Institut).

Mauthner, Fritz (1923): *Wörterbuch der Philosophie*, 1st Vol., 2nd edition, (Leipzig: Meiner).

Practices, Discourses and Politics
of the ›Energetic‹

How to Talk About Energy?
Intangible Scenarios as Epistemic Orders

Barbara Gronau

Notions of Energy

The director Eugenio Barba once stated that an experienced actor only attracts an audience's attention via his body's own energy levels. Admittedly, an actor's charisma alone could also hold the audience in suspense, such as when they witness a purely technical demonstration, e.g. a physical exercise. However, the director also had to acknowledge:

> Speaking of the actor's ›energy‹ means using a term that can cause a thousand misunderstandings. We must give the word ›energy‹ a practical meaning. Etymologically, it has the meaning of ›to be at work‹. But how can the performer's body be at work before it expresses anything? What could we use to replace this word ›energy‹? (Barba 1996: 9)[1]

The recourse to the energetic has appeared in the performing arts for over a hundred years in various constellations, and has only intensified and differentiated itself in recent decades.[2] For example, the Japanese actor Yoshi Oida recommends particular exercises for the development of one's »human energy« (Oida/Marshall 2012: 82-88); the director Peter Brook

---

1 See also: Eugenio Barba (1991) »Energy.« In: Eugenio Barba/Nicola Savarese (eds.): *A Dictionary of Theatre Anthropology. The Secret Art of the Performer*, London/New York, pp. 186-204.

2 Earlier versions of this text in the German language can be found in: Barbara Gronau (ed.) (2012): *Szenarien der Energie*, (Bielefeld: transcript); pp. 111-130; and »Inszenierung und Evidenz. Das Energetische und seine Inszenierungen« online at: https://wissenderkuenste.de/texte/ausgabe-2/inszenierung-und-evidenz-zur-aesthetik-energetischer-phaenomene/ [1.1.2019].

believes in »energies« connecting actors and the audience;[3] and the actor Bernhard Schütz discusses the »energy of a space«, which he, as an actor, has to contend with.[4] Furthermore, Joseph Beuys has crafted an »energy plan for the Western man« (Kuoni 1990), while the performance artist Marina Abramović simply states that: »energy is the goal of my art«.[5] With the concept of »energy«, one attempts to grasp the immaterial and medial conditions of artistic representation, as well as their effects.

With the performative turn of the last few decades, the humanities and cultural sciences have also begun to pay new attention to the question of the energetic. Summarized under the concept of »performativity« (see Fischer-Lichte 2008), this focus reveal that not only texts, monuments and objects, but above all human practices, knowledge and forms of performance are decisive for a culture. Consequently, it has redirected scholarly focus toward the eventful, embodied, and powerful forms of action that permeate all cultures.

Thus the focus of scientific interest has shifted to encompass not only the ephemeral, social, and media exchange processes between actors and spectators, but also their effects. The question of energy therefore represents one of the core questions in art and cultural studies. It initially encompasses the problems of the description and analysis of immaterial and ephemeral constellations: how can this promised and theorized aspect be counted or photographed when, although it is indeed noticeable, it can nonetheless barely be weighed? On the other hand, the term refers also to the technical, traditional, and economic parameters inherent in all artistic production processes. Every operatic aria, every movement or étude, and every brushstroke express the energetic processes of the body. Whether these performances are presented to the audience with flamboyant grandeur or as subdued; with dynamism or with ›modest restraint‹; depends on the historically and culturally varying discourses regarding the body's economy.

---

3 »Any Event Stems from Combustion: Actors, Audiences and Theatrical Energy.« Peter Brook interviewed by Jean Kalman, New Theatre Quarterly 8 (1992), No. 30, pp. 107-112.

4 »Die echte Träne ist wieder in Mode.« Bernhard Schütz in conversation with Stephan Müller. In: Anton Rey/Hajo Kurzenberger/Stephan Müller (eds.) (2011): Wirkungsmaschine Schauspieler. Vom Menschendarsteller zum multifunktionalen Spiel-macher, (Berlin: Alexander Verlag), pp. 53-74, here p. 60.

5 Marina Abramović interviewed by Martina Kaden anlässlich der Verleihung des »BZ Kultur-preises« 2012. BZ, 25.01.2012, p. 26.

Theories of the energetic are therefore also always already being implicitly negotiated, even if the concept does not explicitly appear in corresponding theories of theatrical work. Conversely, the artistic use of the concept of energy is rarely accompanied by a definitive or discursive-critical application. Instead, energy is a term in which scholarly, life-worldly and spiritual imaginations overlap. The most decisive political and ecological upheavals of our time are associated with a reflection upon energetic connections in a globalized world. Despite this inflationary rhetoric, however, any discussion of energy is still subject to a whole series of problems. This is partly due to the fact that »energy« is an *umbrella term* that can refer to wildly differing natural forms, for example: the electric charges of a magnet, the heat of a body, or an object's impulse to move. However, it is also used with life-world or spiritual connotations, through synonyms such as Chi, life energy, aura, or tension. This is by no means a problem of inexact scholarship or the metaphorical use of language; rather, the term is more of a productive void in which the various orders of knowledge intersect with their conceptual applications during a particular time. For example, Johann Heinrich Zedler's *Universal Lexicon (Grosses Universallexikon)* from 1734 defines the keyword Energeia as: »the effect, impact or power of a thing or its spirit« (Zedler 1961: Column 1774). Meyer's *Conversational Lexicon (Konversationslexikon)* of 1908 lists energy as: »the ability to do work« or the »drive« of a character (Meyers 1908: 774). And as late as 1963, the physicist Richard Feynman stated in his famous »Lectures on Physics«:

> It is important to realize that in physics today, we have no knowledge of what energy *is*. We do not have a picture that energy comes in little blobs of a definite amount. [...] However, there are formulas for calculating some numerical quantity, and when we add it all together it gives ›28‹ – always the same number. It is an abstract thing [...].[6]

This is to say: energy implies a purely abstract quantity of conservation, which can only be physically described as a system property. Namely, this means that something exists that nonetheless »never changes, despite any of its

---

6 The Feynman Lectures on Physics, Volume I, Chapter 4 »The Conservation of Energy« are available online at: www.feynmanlectures.caltech.edu/I_04.html.

processes of transformation, it simply remains constant. One can measure this ›something‹ – without actually knowing what it is.« (Kassung 2014: 19)

Therefore, when faced with the question: *How to Talk About Energy?* our initial answer must be: in a radical anti-essentialist way. Energy has no fixed physical characteristics. It cannot be determined ontologically, but rather only in terms of its constellations. In addition to scientific and mathematical methods, it is important to also apply an arts and cultural sciences perspective, which focuses on the slippage between concept and metaphor, between theoretical and practical knowledge, and between the various historical implications of energy. The following four perspectives can be helpful in this endeavor:

1. The first perspective addresses the question of: How can energetic processes become perceptible and evident? The common interpretation of *energy as an »invisible background«* includes the connotation of a force inherent to all things and processes, which must initially be »uncovered« using experimental procedures, technical visualizations or physical performances. Prominent examples include experiments with electricity, which have become popular since the 18th century. In a series of spectacular experiments by Stephen Gray, Georg Bose, Abee Nollet and Michael Faraday, human bodies repeatedly float, twitch and jump while being exposed to electrical charges, demonstrating that they can be moved, dictated or connected by invisible forces.[7] The theatrical character of these experimental arrangements serves above all to generate evidence: via the blinking of the apparatus or the twitching of muscle, the ›underlying‹ force becomes not only visible, but actually physically *real*. The energetic is therefore simultaneously both the condition *and* the effect of these scientific, technical and artistic productions. Any discussion of energy therefore always already entails a consideration of those *scenarios* that frame and exhibit that which is otherwise only fleeting and immaterial.

2. The second perspective interrogates the meaning of *energy as a circulating »in-between« force*, i.e. as a medial and transgressive process that establishes connections between subjects, objects, bodies, thoughts and dis-

---

7   See Arthur Elsenaar, Remko Schar (2002): »Electric Body Manipulation as Performance Art: A Historical Perspective.« *Leonardo Music Journal* 12, pp. 17-28; Oliver Hochadel (2003): *Öffentliche Wissenschaft. Elektrizität in der deutschen Aufklärung*, (Göttingen: Wallstein Verlag).

tant spaces. Whether in the »currents and rays« (Asendorf 1989) of *Fin de Siècle* or in the seemingly utopian fantasies of electric oscillations, all genres – spanning the gamut of romance novels to modern music to science fiction – invoke the idea of ›transgression‹ when referencing the energetic, which itself dissolves boundaries, identities and entities. This does not formulate an esoterically charged longing for community as much as an immanent critique of modernity. In the words of the art historian Christoph Asendorf: »The current is reification's counter image.« (Asendorf 1984: 110)

3. The third perspective inquires about the understanding of *energy as a source of effects*, i.e. as an effecting and transforming force; as a source for the generation of the world. This idea was already well-known during Greek antiquity, when the term »energeia« implied an active doing in the world. With the discovery of thermodynamics during the 19th century, however, this model became counteracted by the idea of entropy, i.e. the realization that every production is at the same time an irreversible loss. Energy cannot be produced, but rather can only ever be converted between forms. The energetic's performative aspects must therefore always be supplemented by the perspective of the elapsing and dissolving of oneself. The ephemerality of theatre is one symbolic representation of this, and the modern arts in particular have established an awareness of the entropic via the dissolution of forms, narratives and structures. The arts have played a decisive role in developing a conceptualization of the body as a system containing an »energy balance«, both at the level of the subject and at the level of aesthetic procedures.

4. The fourth and final perspective investigates *the energetic as implicit or embodied form of knowledge (tacit knowing)* (Polanyi 1966), which is especially prominent in the performing arts. This »knowledge in the arts«[8] entails an embodied, habitualized and commonly held understanding, which is acquired via training and practice. It must be re-adapted to each individual body and scene, and yet often contains no pre-existing or pre-

---

8 »Knowlede in the Arts« means that the arts represent a genuine field for the production, storage and mediation of knowledge. Moreover: the arts themselves can be seen as producers of knowledge as they generate own epistemologies. For further descriptions see the website of our DFG research training group: https://www.udk-berlin.de/en/research/temporary-research-institutes/dfg-research-training-group-knowledge-in-the-arts/ [1.1.2019].

established vocabulary of its own. This unique »knowing of energy« also encompasses the production and reception of performances. It cannot be weighed, counted or photographed, yet is nevertheless an intrinsic part of every theatrical representation as well as its reception by audiences. This perspective evokes a series of questions: What knowledge of energy is generated by the performing arts? Conversely, what influence do the various scientific, technical, and economic discourses on energy have upon the practice of the performing arts? And what role do bodies, materials, sounds, architecture or even the duration of rehearsals and performances play in the development of a specific energy of the theatre?

In contemporary theatre – and here the thesis of this volume comes into play – energetic processes migrate to the centre of artistic practice, bringing these critical questions with them. On the one hand, this becomes apparent in the way that performers deal with their bodies, as they become new testing and experimenting grounds for these energies themselves. On the other hand, this also becomes apparent in the search for new ways to impact the audience, potentially by subjecting them to lengthy durations (of a scene), collective strain, or the fabrication of intense situations. Last but not least, the search for other economies is found within contemporary reflection upon forms of ›artistic work‹. This leads to an interesting historical shift: while avant-garde artists regularly focused upon the utopian aspects of the energetic's dynamics, efficiency and exaggeration during the beginning of the 20th century, neo-avant-garde artists increasingly depicted an interest in the energetic's disturbances, deconstructions or dissolutions of form. *Our perspective on »Energetic Forces as Aesthetic Interventions«* therefore entails: in contemporary productions the energetic no longer merely functions as the condition of an artistic form, but becomes its central object. This practice becomes interventionist when it uncovers and investigates the general conditions of theatrical representation.

In the following analysis, I will outline this process using two examples. The first is related to the field of body economies – more precisely, the artistic critique of efficiency utopias. The second regards making the immaterial perceptible using bodily practices.

Efficiency and Output: Bodily Economies

The phantasm of impending fatigue as the hard limit of human creative power has become one of the foundational rhetorical figures of the 20th century. By 1900 modern discourses of productivity and progress had already begun to develop, and subsequently became seemingly threatened by the discovery of *entropy*. Reflections upon these potential crises are formulated within various *scenarios of deficiency*, which focus upon questions of energy. How long is expenditure possible? What forms and processes does it have? How can it be controlled and modified? Questions such as these inspired the well-known chemist Wilhelm Ostwald to develop a cultural theory from the so-called energetic imperative: »Do not waste energy, rather use it!« (Ostwald 1912: 13) This idea eventually led to schoolchildren in classrooms and soldiers being sprayed with an »anti-fatigue serum« (the so-called »anti-cenotoxin«), which had been developed by putting rats through exercises in order to increase their ability to concentrate (Rabinbach 2001: 170-174). Examples of the application of this imperative extend even to the use of mechanical strength apparatuses, to which working institutes from Berlin to Moscow had strapped proletarian test subjects in the 1920s.

The arts have played a decisive role in the development of a modern economic understanding of the body and its energy balance. For example, an analysis of the Russian avant-garde, offers an exemplary depiction of how a new understanding of acting was developed out of these discourses of work, movement and rationalization – i.e. energy efficiency.[9] It is crucial to note that this logic of progress transformed into almost its exact opposite in many art forms, due to the catastrophes of the Second World War. Even the early »Happenings« and artistic »Actions« of the 1950s ceased searching for motifs or processes of increased efficiency and productivity, but rather began to focus upon contrasting forms of loss and waste.

One example of this is the well-known »24 Hour Happening«, organized by gallery owner Rudolf Jährling in Wuppertal on June 5, 1965.[10] The

---

9 See also Barbara Gronau (2007): »Die Energie des Theaters.« In: *fundiert – Wissenschafts-magazin der FU Berlin*, June 2007, online at: https://www.fu-berlin.de/presse/publikationen/fundiert/archiv/2007_01/07_01_gronau/gronau.pdf

10 Bazon Brock published a programme of these Happenings, available online at: https://bazonbrock.de/werke/detail/?id=2982&sectid=3305; See also: Barbara Gronau (2016): »Die Zeit aufführen. Zur Kunst der Long Durational Performance.« In: Michael Gamper/Eva

participating artists included Joseph Beuys, Bazon Brock, Charlotte Moorman, Nam June Paik, Eckart Rahn, Tomas Schmit and Wolf Vostell, who gathered for a period of 24 hours to create a series of »Happenings« or »Actions« in the gallery owner's villa. Vostell stuck thousands of pins into fresh cattle entrails. Paik staged a 24-hour *concert* with naked plastic-wrapped cellist Charlotte Moorman. The musician Eckart Rahn undertook a live setting of the Kinsey Report with double bass and recorder. Bazon Brock meditated on a conference table, either while standing or lying on his head. Tomas Schmit performed his *Action Without an Audience* by emptying the water in a series of buckets, one into the other, cyclically. Beuys squatted, stood and acted upon a small crate of oranges for the duration of his piece. »Looking back,« reflects the artist Bazon Brock, »our theme was the constitution of a 24 hour period via these Happenings.«[11]

What became clear in this early example of a long durational performance[12] is not only the process-related and dynamic nature of action art, but also the moment of its self-dissolution. After several hours the organizer acquiesced all control over the space; pain and instances of weakness spread throughout the group; actors left the field; audience members slept in the corners; and the action ended after 23 hours due to general exhaustion. Therefore, the »Happenings« demonstrates the staging of not only artistic forms, but also of their energetic conditions. For example: after several hours Vostell's maltreated beef began to rot and stink; Schmit's buckets of water continuously decreased in volume; and Beuys' gestures became increasingly shaky.

The forms examined here all exist under the condition of entropy, and illustrate what Rudolf Arnhem once called the »catabolic effect« of entropic growth (Neswald 2006), i.e. the destruction of form or the loss of voltage

---

Geulen/Johannes Grave/Andreas Langenohl/Ralf Simon/Sabine Zubarik (eds.): *Zeit der Form – Formen der Zeit,* (Hannover: Wehrhahn Verlag), pp.173-186.

11 Bazon Brock cited in: Uwe Schneede (1994): *Joseph Beuys. Die Aktionen. Kommentiertes Verzeichnis mit fotografischen Dokumentationen,* (Stuttgart: Hatje Cantz) p. 84.

12 »The term ›durational‹ is often used […] to indicate an art work that draws attention to its temporal constraint as a constitutive element of its meaning. The meaning of the word duration itself, evolving from the Latin *duratus* (to last), is bound into the notion of persistence, of remaining through time, and is separable from but shadowed by the term endurance, often associated with sufferance.« Adrian Heathfield (2009): *Out of Now: The Lifeworks of Tehching Hsieh,* (London and Cambridge: MIT Press), p. 22.

Figure 1: *24 Hour Happening*. Charlotte Moorman sleeping.

Figure 2: *24 Hour Happening*. Audience.

over time (Arnheim 1979: 43). The peculiarity of *long durational performances* lies in the experience of what could be called the »forces of time«, especially in terms of the entropy always ensuring that a form's emergence is visibly and equally accompanied by its dissolution. These performances open up qualitative experiences beyond metric caesuras by presenting themselves as physical stress, as energetic fluctuation, or as a state of crisis.

To build upon this example, I would also conversely like to recall the tendencies of ectropy[13] (the opposite of entropy) and waste that have developed in the contemporary performative arts. Above all, these include scenes in which the body visibly expends its energy via excessive movements, such as: long periods of standing without moving; holding itself in an unbalanced position; rhythmic pounding and screaming; a permanent repetition of the same movement; or also running, climbing, sliding or dancing to the point of complete exhaustion. In such instances, the logic of *homo economicus*, normally oriented toward »scarcity, lack, infinite striving, and productive, consumerist work,« (Vogl 2004: 345) becomes reversed, and instead now celebrates the losing and excessive spending of.

One example of this inversion is found in the piece *Schwalbe Performs on their Own* by the Dutch troupe *Schwalbe*, as performed in 2010 at the ENTROPIA festival.[14] In what was declared to be a »CO_2-neutral performance«, eight performers entered a completely dark and cold stage and removed their underclothes, which had been purchased second hand. Initially audience members could only hear the soft humming of pedals, until a moment later a strong spotlight flooded the performers with a glistening light. Eight men and women were then revealed to be sitting on home exercise equipment of various sizes and designs. They were cycling in a breathtaking manner, silently staring at the audience with tremendous focus. The power, generated by their leg muscles via pedaling, flowed from the sports equipment directly into their headlamps – this not only illuminated the scenery, but also created it.

---

13 Ectropy (Ectropia) is a concept coined by, and defined as »the tendency to increase the state of order of a living system via assimilation.« It is considered to be the opposite of entropy. See: Helmuth Plessner (1975): *The Stages of the Organic and the Human*, 3rd edition, (Berlin: de Gruyter).

14 *Schwalbe Performs on their Own*, directed by Lotte van den Berg, Netherlands 2010. For video and further information see: www.schwalbe.nu/voorstellingen/4 [1.1.2019].

One could only hear the high squeaking, humming, and clattering of the mounted fitness equipment. When the audience's inevitable voyeurism towards the half-naked actors finally ebbed, it quickly became apparent that there was nothing more to be seen here than the collective expenditure of eight averagely trained bodies. What at first appeared to be a gentle cycling exercise has somehow transformed into an arduous marathon, and none of the actors seem to be able to stop.

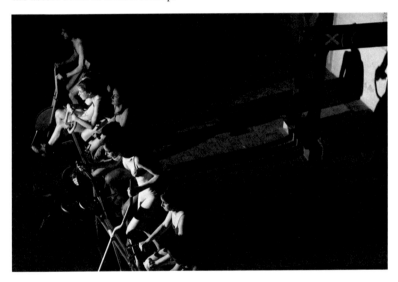

Figure 3: *Schwalbe Performs on their Own* (2010), directed by Lotte van den Berg.

The longer the scene lasted, the less pleasant each position obviously became. The actors began to show symptoms of weakening forces: red-hot thighs, thick streams of sweat, and the wobbling of their upper bodies to the left and right. Here, for the entertainment of the audience, actors literally »broke their own backs« for almost an hour. Later on, one performer swiveled the spotlight to ›do a lap‹ around the room, the glistening light encompassed not only the cyclers, but also the walls and audience. Suddenly illuminated as part of the scene, observers were left feeling uneasily coopted by this theatrical focus. The omission of any narration, figures, or plot cast the audience back to the naked economy of the theatre itself: namely to exchange money for a performance. As each performer, having reached the end of his strength, abandoned his or her exercise machine, the light became weaker. In the agonizing finale of the performance, the final performer held her own body like a lighthouse against the spreading darkness – until this single source of energy was also finally extinguished.

This performance is perhaps the strongest juxtaposition to the exchange-based economy of the so-called bourgeois theatre, in which it was frowned upon for physical effort to be visible on stage. Instead, only a style exuding effortlessness and self-control was considered admirable. In contrast, performance today seems to be a matter of showing an audience that energy is transformed, in other words: that *work* is being done here. With the disappearance of physical labor during the age of the service society, effort is transferred to the realm of art. A longing for radical exertion contains the symptomatic transfer of the gesture of work from the social to the aesthetic. One could say: at the end of efficiency stands the triumph of defeat. In addition, theatre itself becomes a research laboratory, in which the course and limits of one's physical ability to perform and also suffer are examined. Here too is the materiality of the body or voice playfully examined, while its effects upon an audience are tested. This energy of the theatre evokes aesthetic experiences, which themselves run through the bodies of both performers and observers. The audience therefore leaves the Schwalbe groups' performance somehow also exhausted.

Perceptions of the Intangible: Spectacular Body Experiments

Building upon this metaphoric scenario of a research laboratory and the principle of transmission, my last example addresses how artistic practices make invisible energies both evident and perceptible.

In 1973, the Austrian artist Valie Export staged a performance in her Vienna studio entitled *Hyperbulie*. The materials used included a »corridor of electrically charged wire, batteries, and a person.«[15] Cameraman Hermann Hendrich's black-and-white recordings on both video and photo depict a bare, cellar-like room, in which long wires of varying heights are stretched to form a narrow corridor. Two Tudor brand car batteries charge the wires,

---

15 See: Valie Export in Anita Prammer (1988): *Valie Export. Eine multimediale Künstlerin*, (Wien: Wiener Frauenbuchverlag).

and the word »Hyperbulie« is written in chalk on the bare wooden floor. The naked artist enters the scene from the left, and moves between the wires within the next seven minutes – first standing upright, then increasingly contorted, and finally crawling. As she moves, she forces herself to touch the wires (with her cheek, shoulder, and knee), which electrocute her every time. However, the effects of her inevitable pain are almost invisible in this piece: Export's body does not twitch or tremble. Rather, what can be witnessed is a woman who is slowly working her way through an increasingly strenuous exercise, namely: deliberate self-injury from the electrical charges, as a result of which (depending on the intensity, type and point of entry) muscle paralysis, ventricular fibrillation and burns could result.

Figure 4: Valie Export: *Hyperbulie* (Vienna, 1973).

The title *Hyperbulie* brings this piece into the realm of the pathological: defined as psychotically induced action or the manic urge to act. It appears to be about the overcoming of oneself in a way that exceeds norms, or rather about a way of enduring against physical injury within the framework of an artistic setting. The goal of this setting – as Export explains in a text accompanying the piece – is to illuminate social constraints and restrictions.

The electric corridor represents the »[...] closed, structured space of society, which dispenses and regulates all human energy via painful barriers, so that man [...] becomes a tamed animal who ultimately collapses [...]« (Export 1992: 212-213).

Export's piece can be located within the wide realm of Body-Art examples, in which the targeted evocation of pain and danger can also simultaneously be conceived as an act of *self-elevation*. As the art historian Rosemarie Brucher has recently shown, artists like Export thus follow an »aesthetics of the sublime«, informed by Kant and Schiller, which identifies, within the controlled self-endangerment of the subject, a simultaneous recuperating of its own autonomy (Brucher 2013). This essay must bracket the many interesting aspects that arise about the legacies of such philosophical models, as, in this reading, Export's example is not primarily about pain, but rather the energetic current.

In Export's setting, electricity performs at least three different functions. (1) It is less the object of action than a partner in that action. The artist performs a type of *pathway* in which her movements are determined by a highly effective force which possesses the ability to move, to steer, to hurt, to burn, or even to kill the subject. (2) Electricity is paradoxically an invisible »backdrop« here, because its actual interaction with the actor remains invisible to us. Neither the current itself nor its physical effects *reveal* themselves to the outside observer. Rather, the responsibility of proving that something is indeed occurring before our eyes, albeit invisibly, is assumed to a greater extent by the surrounding setting: (i.e. the wire constellation, the car batteries' logo, the camera recording the scene, the title chalked on the floor, and the accompanying text). One of the most irritating sensations experienced by the film's audience is in fact the unspectacular dynamic of the piece's action, or rather the lack thereof. Only once does the audience suspect they hear the artist's slightly groaning exhalation, as she repeatedly brushes up against the wire with her face. Of course, even this concealment of pain is an intrinsic part of the moment of »endurance«[16] in Body Art. (3) The nature of this event can best be described using the concept of transmission: electricity flows (transfers) out of the metal and into the body, and then back again. It

---

16 Building upon the term ›Body Art‹, the term ›Endurance Art‹ not only marks the body as an object of artistic action, but also a method of addressing it, and is oriented towards endurance and self-overcoming. See: *Performing Arts Journal* 54, 18/3 (1996) pp. 66-70.

therefore connects two diversities into a new unity: namely by forming an electrical circuit in which the naked body functions as a so-called »ohmic resistance«. In addition, the artist performs an act of literary transference, as she applies electricity as a political metaphor in her accompanying text, and compares it to human society. Interestingly, this use of metaphor appears paradoxical, because electricity represents the painful regulation of a parceled-out society on the one hand, while also indicating the »free flowing energies« of a self-liberated subject on the other. Finally, this transfer also extends to the audience, who unexpectedly find themselves using the medium of film to create their own imagined reproductions of the event.

On these three levels – immateriality, mediality and efficacy – the piece *Hyperbulie* paradigmatically demonstrates what I would like to call an »energy scenario«. These are the scenic, even theatrical arrangements of invisible forces, for the purpose of one's own exploration, experience and engagement. In her compilation of »Wire, Battery, Man« Export invokes an almost three-hundred-year tradition of physical experiments, ranging from Galvanis' work on twitching frog legs, to Otto von Guerecke's electrostatic machines, and finally to Benjamin Franklin's lightning conductor. These experiments on bodies sought to make invisible forces and their effects observable. The experimental object – i.e. the knowledge of energetic forms and functions – is similarly generated in Body-Art via a performance, but one that is now enacted upon and through one's own body.

Conclusion

It seems to me that the question »*How to Talk About Energy?*« can hardly be answered without looking at the performing arts. The energetic can never be seen directly, but rather only perceived via the lenses of various scenarios that frame and exhibit that which is otherwise fleeting and immaterial. In other words: the energetic is both a condition and product of scholarly, technical and artistic productions. Theatrical practices have played an important role in establishing and disseminating scientific discourses on energy. Conversely, various historical conceptions and theories of the energetic are reflected in the respective performing arts of their time. In order to outline a theatrical concept of energy, praxeological and phenomenological approaches will be required, in addition to standard discourse-analysis methods. As the energetic is founded on a collective experience of being alive, an examination of contemporary theatre can be fruitful here. This is because the energetic becomes the center of artistic practice, particularly via the way the performers deal with their bodies in their search for new ways to impact the audience, as well as in the dialectic of generation and disappearance. Any discussion of energy therefore also entails considering this key concept of human culture, which itself reveals epistemic upheavals in human understandings of both the world and self.

Works Cited

Arnheim, Rudolf (1979): *Kunst und Entropie*, (Köln: DuMont).
Asendorf, Christoph (1984): *Batterien der Lebenskraft. Zur Geschichte der Dinge und ihrer Wahrnehmung im 19. Jahrhundert*, (Gießen: VDG Weimar).
Asendorf, Christoph (1989): *Ströme und Strahlen. Das langsame Verschwinden der Materie um 1900*, (Gießen: Anabas).
Barba, Eugenio (1996): »Wiederkehrende Prinzipien.« In: Pfaff, Walter/Keil, Erika/Schläpfer, Beat (eds.): *Der sprechende Körper. Texte zur Theateranthropologie*, (Berlin: Alexander Verlag), pp. 77-97.
Brucher, Rosemarie (2013): *Subjektermächtigung und Naturunterwerfung. Künstlerische Selbstverletzung im Zeichen von Kants Erhabenem*, (Bielefeld: transcript).
Export, Valie (1992): »Hyperbulie.« In: *Valie Export. Katalog Oberösterreichisches Landesmuseum*, (Linz: Spirit Media), pp. 212-213.
Fischer-Lichte, Erika (2008): *The Transformative Power of Performance: A New Aesthetics*, (New York: Routledge).
Kassung, Christian (2014): »Was bleibt und was nicht bleibt. Eine sehr kurze Geschichte der Energie.« In: Barbara Gronau (ed.): *Szenarien der Energie. Zur Ästhetik und Wissenschaft des Immateriellen*, (Bielefeld: transcript), pp. 15-23.
Kuoni, Carin (ed.) (1990): *Joseph Beuys in America: Energy Plan for the Western Man*, (New York: Four Walls Eight Windows).
Meyers (1908): *Meyers großes Konversations-Lexikon*, 5 Vols, (Leipzig und Wien: Bibliographisches Institut).
Neswald, Elizabeth R. (2006): *Thermodynamik als kultureller Kampfplatz. Zur Faszinationsgeschichte der Entropie 1850-1915*, (Freiburg: Rombach Verlag).

Yoshi Oida, Yoshi/Marshall, Lorna (2012): *Der unsichtbare Schauspieler*, (Berlin: Alexander Verlag).

Ostwald, Wilhelm (1912): *Der energetische Imperativ*, (Leipzig: Akademische Verlagsgesellschaft).

Polanyi, Michael (1966): *The Tacit Dimension*, (Chicago/London: University of Chicago Press).

Rabinbach, Anson (2001): *Motor Mensch. Energie, Ermüdung und die Ursprünge der Modernität*, (Wien: Turia und Kant Verlag).

Rey, Anton/Kurzenberger, Hajo/Müller, Stephan (eds.) (2011): *Wirkungsmaschine Schauspieler. Vom Menschendarsteller zum multifunktionalen Spiel-macher*, (Berlin: Alexander Verlag).

Vogl, Joseph (2004): *Kalkül und Leidenschaft. Poetik des ökonomischen Menschen*, (Zürich und Berlin: Diaphanes Verlag).

Zedler, Johann Heinrich (1961): *Grosses vollständiges Universal-Lexicon aller Wissenschaften und Künste 1731-1754*, Vol. 8, (Graz: Akademische Druck- und Verlagsanstalt), Column 1774.

Dancing the Energy/Energizing the Dancing

Susan Leigh Foster

At one point in *Pichet Klunchun et Moi* (2005), a duet choreographed by Jérôme Bel, Klunchun observes that European classical dance is always throwing energy away. In contrast, his own training in Thai classical dance has taught him that curved hands, arms, feet, and legs are shaped so as to recycle energy, and direct it back in towards the center of the body. He illustrates this analysis by contrasting a sequence of grand jetés, replete with arms and legs thrusting out in unison on each leap, with a slower phrase of Thai steps in which arms and legs are raised but always in careful arcs that create a sphere-like space around the body.[1] Klunchun's comments direct our attention to the ways that energy is conceptualized and also channeled or managed. They also ask us to consider how both the choreography of a particular form and the training regimens or other kinds of preparation necessary to perform it approach and handle energy.

Rudolf Laban has offered us a powerful analysis of energy and its connection to space and time, as well as to psychological states. He shows how, for example, the free or bound flow of energy conveys different meanings and signals states of being for the dancer or danced character.[2] However,

---

1 This description of Klunchun's performance is based upon two separate viewings of *Pichet Klunchun et Moi* which I saw, one at Dance Theater Workshop, November 8, 2007 and the second at the Disney-Redcat Theater, February 27, 2009. The duet toured internationally for several years.

2 For English language explanations of Laban's conceptualizations of space, time, and flow, see Irmgard Bartenieff and Dori Lewis (1980): *Body Movement: Coping with the Environment* (New York: Gordon and Breach); and Decily Dell (1975): *A Primer for Movement Description Using Effort/Shape*, (New York: Dance Notation Bureau). Additional analyses of the relationship between patterns of energy used in moving and psychological states can be found in Warren Lamb (1965): *Posture and Gesture: An Introduction to the Study of Physical Behavior*,

the analysis that follows will take a different approach. Drawing inspiration from Klunchun's observation, it will focus more on how energy is conceptualized in different dance traditions, and also on how energy and the body mutually define one another.

For any given dance practice, is the body a force, a flow, a structure, or an organism? Does energy fuel, feed, or animate the body? Is the body a field of energy that shifts from moment to moment? How do preparations for dancing address energy and what kind of relationship do they construct between the body learning to dance in the studio and the body performing dance onstage? Answers to these questions might be found in the vocabulary and sequencing of movement, the ways a dancer learns to engage with viewers, and the ways that bodies interact with each other. Evidence could equally be found in pedagogical practices associated with a given form: the ways that prompts, exercises, tasks, or other forms of preparation are organized and presented, the verbal descriptions offered to guide students towards a more ideal performance, and the organization of the dance class itself. Throughout all these phases of learning and performing dance, ideas are promulgated about the body and energy, their organization and function.

In the analysis that follows, I approach the practice of dancing as an activity that embodies a theory of bodily energy and how it operates. In the very ways that a given dance practice is organized and transmitted from one dancer to another, any given practice pursues a hypothetical vision of what energy is. It elaborates this vision through the metaphors, articulated in both words and movements, that are implemented to assert the body's identity while dancing. Each form of dance proposes a series of »what ifs«: *what if* the body is a vessel, a vehicle, an instrument that is mobilized by energy? Or *what if* dance movement creates energy that is beautiful, ideal, or natural? These »what ifs« form a relatively consistent and coherent whole through which the dance form itself is constructed, and into which the dancer enters as part of that construction.

When I dance, whether onstage or in a bar, I am aware that it requires energy: demanding effort and exertion that can eventually leave me breathless, fatigued, and sometimes unable to move for a while. However, I am also aware that dancing generates energy, making me exuberant, buoyant,

---

(London: Gerald Duckworth, 1965) and also Warren Lamb and Elizabeth Watson (1979): *Body Code: The Meaning in Movement*, (London: Routledge and Kegan Paul).

enthusiastic, and generally excited about what might come next. Taking a cue from this introspective observation, this essay focuses specifically on assumptions around the amount of energy available to the body, asking whether for any given dance practice energy is treated as scarce or abundant. Is energy reliably available and ever present? Or is it something that must be carefully managed and strategically directed so as to ensure its availability? Is it even something to be concerned about, or tapped into; cultivated or simply enjoyed?

I will focus on three distinctive dance practices – classical ballet, somatics, and contact improvisation – and will offer a very brief portrait of each that focuses on how each manages, directs, or relies upon energy. All three forms draw from medical and scientific research on the body, making evident the extent to which sciences of and about the body have profoundly influenced the ways that it is conceptualized. Each practice, however, makes very different use of these insights in terms of how energy is utilized. All three forms have also changed significantly over time, so that my observations – purposefully pitched at a very general level of analysis – may very well not hold up when examining a specific practitioner, whether choreographer, teacher, or dancer, or a given moment within the historical development of practice. Still, I hope they will illustrate some of the kinds of insights into dancing that an inquiry into energy might yield. My discussion will draw from my experiences as a student of the practices and as a viewer of them.

Classical Ballet

Classical ballet offers a highly systematic approach to training the body, one that cultivates energy through the methodical, logical progressions of steps and phrases that are sequenced according to difficulty. The mastery of each set of steps inculcates skills that then serve as the basis for access to the next level of accomplishment. The steadily expanding repertoire of skills aims to build physical prowess, while at the same time instilling in the body the basic aesthetic features of the form. Although there are many variations on how the curriculum is structured, each works to provide the most effective sequencing for building up the body in terms of strength, coordination, flexibility, and dexterity. The clear progression of skillsets conveys the sense that energy is something the body uses, but also something that can be enhanced and expanded.

At each level of the curriculum's progression, basic phrases are taught whose syntax for the sequences of steps typically involves moments of lesser and greater emphasis. This creates a sense that some movements are climactic and others are transitional; some movements impress themselves especially and are seen as the pinnacle of achievement, whereas others assist in building towards or otherwise preparing for these special moments. Often, phrases are also repeated multiple times as if to re-emphasize the difficulty and importance of specific moments within them. This phrasing of movement sequences, along with the clear progression of skills that the student acquires, creates the impression that energy is carefully modulated so as to imprint forcefully on the viewer certain key positions and steps, and most often these are moments of extreme extension, precarious balance, or lofty height. The extensions, balances, jumps, and leaps progress in difficulty as the student moves from being a beginner to an advanced dancer.

At the same time, the performance of all movements must look easy and undemanding, with the performer exuding a light and buoyant confidence. The effort and the energy it takes to accomplish any given feat must be masked, and this is taught in classes through the establishment of a serene and pleasant facial expression and a smooth quality in the execution of all steps and phrases. Effortlessness is also built into the very positioning and phrasing of each step and sequence of steps; the ways that head, arms, torso, and legs are angled and shaped in their motions so as to appear both easy and precise. Certain positions and steps, perceived as the most significant, or reflecting the highest achievement and virtuosity, should be targeted with an extra dose of energy that makes them more impactful, but they should still appear effortless. When performed expertly these same moves seem to energize the dancer; the sense of accomplishment imparts a satisfaction and delight – often registered in the dancers' facial expressions – that seems to drive them towards greater accomplishments, all in pursuit of an ideal beauty.

A potent contradiction, which both dancers and viewers accept, is thus built into ballet's fundamental aesthetic commitment to the appearance of ease. Movements are exhausting yet must appear easy; movements frequently require a considerable exertion of strength yet they must look as though almost no energy was expended. Acceptance of this ruse sustains the image of dance as wondrously special in comparison with other physical pursuits and, equally, that those dancers who excel at ballet are likewise exceptional. Beginning in the latter part of the 20th century, both choreographers and dancers started to make more evident the amount of effort and energy that the dancing demands, resulting in a new style of execution and a new respect, on the part of viewers, for the »hard work« of dancing. This is one notable way that ballet has changed in the last decades.

Over the same period of time, other forms of training that focus specifically on expanding aerobic capacity and strengthening the body in a balanced way have also begun to be tapped to supplement ballet pedagogy. Many curricula now rely on and incorporate the latest findings from medical and scientific research into bodily functioning in order to maximize the energy available for dancing. Anatomy and kinesiology are consulted in order to determine the most effective ways to achieve the aesthetics of the form, including the expansion of flexibility, the turn-out of the legs, and the lightness of landing from jumps and leaps. Sports science is also being adapted to analyze a given dancer's weaknesses or proclivities, to provide physical therapies for injuries, and to retrain the body so as to avoid such injuries in the future. Slow motion videos of jumps or turns provide insight into a give dancer's capacities and limitations and direct both teacher and student towards the specific corrections necessary to improve performance.

These various scientific discourses assist in ›powering up‹ the body: expanding its capacity for and access to energy so that it can move through ever more demanding steps and phrases, sustaining virtuoso performances for longer and longer periods of time. The discourses work synergistically with the curriculum to create a sense that energy is a necessary resource that can be enlarged through effective training. Energy should then be dispensed strategically in order to emphasize certain movements as well as the underlying skills that make them possible. Through this effective deployment of energy, a dancer can secure a virtuoso performance. Ballet itself can also convey its aesthetic investment in certain movements and ways of moving, teaching viewers what is important and what matters within the dance.

Somatics

Somatics is used here to refer to the broad spectrum of training regimens that includes: Body-Mind Centering, devised by Bonnie Bainbridge Cohen; Skinner Release Technique; and Alexander Technique, among others, which often synthesizes some of these techniques into a single pedagogical approach.[3] Despite their many differences, these forms of bodily training share several basic goals: a dedication to uncovering and realizing a ›natural‹ body, an investment in an anatomical understanding of the body's basic structure, and a prioritization of an economical and efficient way of moving. Like ballet, somatics focuses on two related strategies for managing energy, one based in imagery and the other in the medical sciences, specifically anatomy. However, it cultivates these two discourses in ways that are quite different from ballet.

Rather than offering a clear progression of skills that all bodies should assimilate, each body in somatics is seen as unique and capable of a distinctive way of moving. One purpose of instruction is to enable all dancers to access their own individual capacities and unique styles of moving, and to actualize to the fullest the singular and distinctive potential within their physical structure. At the same time, the study of anatomy is essential because it provides fundamental and seemingly universal knowledge of how each joint moves, a capacity that all bodies, it is assumed, share.

A tacit underlying assumption within the various branches of somatics envisions bodies as becoming distorted through habitualized patterns within daily life, along with any training regimens, including other forms of dance training, in which dancers have engaged. Study of anatomy provides an understanding of how parts of the body can and should move; the use

---

3 For an introduction to the work of Cohen, see Bonnie Bainbridge Cohen (1993): *Sensing, Feeling, and Action: The Experiential Anatomy of Body-Mind Centering*, Lisa Nelson and Nancy Stark Smith, (eds.): (Northampton, Ma: Contact Editions). For an introduction to Skinner Technique, see Joan Skinner (1999): »Skinner Releasing Technique,« in Nancy Allinson (ed.): *The Illustrated Encyclopedia of Body-Mind Disciplines*, (New York: Rosen Publishing Group), pp. 265-267; and also Joan Skinner, Bridget Davis, Robert Davidson, Kris Wheeler, and Sally Metcalf, »Skinner Releasing Technique: Imagery and its Application to Movement Training. *Contact Quarterly*, Vol.1 Fall 1979. The literature on Frederick Matthias Alexander is quite extensive, and I refer the reader here only to his original publication: Frederick Matthias Alexander (1923): *Constructive Conscious Control of the Individual*, (New York: E.P. Dutton).

of various prompts based in different imagery about the body is designed to unravel the distortional habits that dancers have acquired. The imagery works to dissolve tensions and to expand dancers' conscious awareness of how the body can move in the most easeful and efficient way.

The process of undoing harmful habits is seen as one that recovers a ›natural‹ body, leading to a natural way of moving. Considerable time is spent in somatics classes focusing on minute movements in designated parts of the body as a way both to unlock or unravel habitualized movement. By intensively scrutinizing a given vertebra or section of the rib cage, for example, dancers can first deconstruct distortional patterning and then slowly build new movement sequences that free up the joints, enabling them to move with ease. By invoking metaphors such as the »spine as smoke« or the »pelvis as a pool of water«, teachers direct students to a level of proprioceptive awareness that equips them both to discover anew and re-pattern their bodies.

In the process of establishing this natural body, dancers learn an anatomically correct way of moving but also, and most significantly from the perspective of this inquiry, an economical way of moving. Even though the goal is not to copy their movement precisely, the style of moving modeled by teachers, along with the imagery given in the somatics class, focuses on utilizing energy efficiently. The dancer should infuse movement with no more energy than is essential to accomplishing a given motion. Energy is seen as naturally available but as needing to be dispensed with the minimum effort required to accomplish the movement task. The reasons for this economy are seldom addressed. Possibly the moderate use of energy is linked to the goal of a more healthful utilization of the body, leading to the inference that somatics offers a superior understanding of how the body should move.

Thus in contrast to ballet where kinesiology and sports science are applied in order to power up the body, somatics focuses largely on the study of anatomy as illuminating the origin of movement that will then flow directly out of anatomical structure, without the need for enhancement. Also – and in contrast to ballet where the vocabulary, facial expression, and style of movement combine to mask the effort it takes to perform many movements – somatics foregrounds the ease with which any and all movement should be performed. All movement takes on a kind of liquid quality in which no movement is emphasized or highlighted more than any other. Rather than flash an explosive energy at the height of a leap or in the sharply composed stance that ends a long series of turns, dancers exude an evenness of energy, seeming never to exert more than the minimum necessary to accomplish any movement phrase.

Also unlike ballet, which is very rarely sourced as a vocabulary for improvised performance, somatics has enjoyed a history, both as a set of principles that can guide and inform improvised performance, and as a regimen for dancers who might use it as a fundamental training program that supports the performance of many different types of choreography created prior to performance. When used as the base for improvised performance, movement seems to generate from and play across the body, articulating the patterning that somatics develops, while at the same time the dancer seeks to discover new and unanticipated sequencing that takes the natural body in new directions. The focus of the improvised choreography is typically the process of discovery itself. When choreographers work with dancers trained in somatics on pieces with pre-set choreography, they might wish to explore a variety of topics that may or may not focus on the parameters established for the natural body. This could include the expression of emotional states and progressions, the relating of narratives with characters, or the staging of encounters between dancers that focus on conflict, desire, or a host of other interactions. Whether they are exploring movement through improvisation or enacting characters or dramas, however, dancers trained in somatics typically adhere to an economy of effort. This tends to convey the sense that movement's efficient execution is as important as any other types of messages that it might encode. Thus, when dancers convey emotional fervency or accomplish striking feats of balance, turning, or falling to the floor, they do so only within the limits of an economical outlay of energy.

In the 1960s – the early years of development for many somatics pedagogies – the orientation of most programs was therapeutic, and worked to help dancers who were otherwise unable to go on dancing return to their careers. As somatics became more widespread, its pedagogies became more streamlined, with standard sets of directives and even exercises replacing the more idiosyncratic and individualized exploration of the conjunction between imagery and anatomy. Although efficiency of motions was always a goal, it has become more pronounced now that so many dancers' bodies register its training. According to Doran George (2014), this has resulted in a more anonymous sense of who any dancer is or what matters to them.[4]

Contact Improvisation

Although contact improvisation is sometimes included as a branch of somatics training, I consider it separately here, specifically because of the different cultivation of energy that it undertakes. Unlike ballet with its clear progression of exercises leading to the acquisition of skills, and more akin to somatics, contact improvisation focuses on opening the body to new forms of sensation that will expand its potential to engage in sharing weight. These ways of moving are directed by certain principles, but they do not form a vocabulary of positions and steps from which phrases of movement are built. Instead, what is possible through implementing contact improvisation's central principles is always unique and yet to be discovered, because there are endless ways that weight sharing can occur. Thus energy is not utilized in order to accomplish specific tasks, but instead directed towards exploration of a limitless unknown. As with improvisers working according to somatics' directives, contact improvisation's exploration often *is* the choreography itself. However, unlike somatics, contact improvisation demonstrates little interest in economy or efficiency, but instead revels in engagement with others.

Especially in its formative years, as Cynthia Novack (1990) points out, contact improvisation cultivated touch and the sensation of weight, converting the body into a mass with the potential for energy to flow across it and merge with whatever surfaces it came into contact. Unlike ballet, there was no conception of center and periphery, nor was there a privileging of uprightness. Any and all parts of the body were equally capable of bearing weight and coming into contact with the floor or with other bodies. Similar to somatics, the practice cultivated a seamless transfer of energy across parts of the body, but in contrast to it, the focus was not on integrating actions of the various joints, but rather on maintaining and exploring a moving point of contact with other surfaces.

---

4 George's dissertation is one of the most comprehensive studies of somatics that has yet been conducted. See Doran George (2014): »A Conceit of the Natural Body: The Universal-Individual in Somatic Dance Training.« (PhD, University of California: Los Angeles).

Steve Paxton, one of the practitioners who helped to develop contact improvisation, emphasized the importance of allowing reflexes, rather than willful intention, to govern the next moment's movement. The idea, both literally and figuratively, was to ›go with the flow‹. Configuring the body as flow, contact improvisation, like the other practices discussed here, also has had recourse to scientific discourses to assist in explaining the practice. However, instruction typically invokes references to physics rather than the biological or medical sciences. The body is likened to a fulcrum or to a momentum rather than an anatomical structure or metabolic entity.

Furthermore, the flow of energy is conceptualized as interactive, merging with the energy of other bodies, and even with the air or floor. When in contact with another body, the goal is to blend energies so completely that the two bodies become defined by the changing point of contact between them. Thus, unlike both ballet and somatics, which focus on the individual as a distinctive entity, contact improvisation is concerned with energy as a productive dynamic that, itself, takes control of and synthesizes the two bodies into a single force whose physical responses to momentum, in combination with the effects of gravity, govern the action.

In order to prepare for this kind of engagement with other bodies, students learn to privilege their sense of touch, and thus to significantly expand their ability to take in the amount and kinds of information that it offers. They soften their visual focus in order to place less importance on visual information, and they dismantle hierarchies trained into the body that organize it into up and down, in and out, backwards and forwards etc. All these approaches to reworking the body contribute to a responsiveness grounded in touch that can also move in any and all directions with equal facility.

In addition to classes in contact improvisation, one of the principle forms of instruction has been the contact jam: an open-ended, informal opportunity for people with different levels of knowledge about the practice to come together and interact spontaneously with one another. Novack makes clear that in the early years these jams could go on for many hours, and they also evolved out of and dissolved back into a communal approach to living and sharing (1990: 63-84). The fact that so few limits are placed on the jam is one indication of the way that energy is seen as amply available. With an unregulated amount of time given to any interaction, dancers are able to explore seemingly without end the infinite possibilities for moving that the directives suggest.

Even once contact improvisation developed more theatrical versions of itself, the sense of open-ended inquiry has remained. Dancers typically appear relaxed yet alert, ready and willing to spring into action at any moment. They evince no effort to exert the minimal amount of energy, as is seen in somatics. Instead they most often demonstrate a willingness to follow wherever touch and momentum are leading, using whatever energy is necessary. The practice of contact improvisation does not appear to be effortless in the way that ballet does, nor does it appear to be regulated for efficiency as in somatics. Instead, energy is simply tapped and used as needed.

At the same time, contact improvisation's emphasis on connecting with another body dissolves the boundedness of the body, transforming it from a self-regulating and self-contained entity into a force-field whose boundaries are constantly changing. Furthermore, as bodies engage and merge in contact, they create energy together synergistically. Thus the amount of energy seemingly expended does not equate to the amount of motion or momentum produced, due to the unpredictable changes in direction and flow produced by gravity working in conjunction with the physical mechanics of the newly configured ›body‹: one with four legs, four arms, two heads, and two torsos. The disorientation and dis-establishment of individuality that results from these encounters sometimes endures even after bodies separate. As a result, a particularly successful jam might yield a kind of energy that permeates all bodies, even those who are there to view the action rather than participate in it.

What Energy? Whose Energy?

Reflecting back on the analysis offered thus far, what kinds of insights seem to be yielded up by using energy as a lens through which to look at dance in general and these practices in particular? It seems, first of all, that a focus on energy contributes new insights to any choreographic analysis, suggesting that readings of dance based in the codes associated with parts of the body, distances between bodies, or relationships to music or to narrative can be expanded to encompass the ways that energy production and management convey meaning. Dance transmits meaning through its utilization of energy and also through the ways that energy is seen to define or interact with the body.

How energy interacts with or passes through the body literally helps to construct what bodily identity is and thus what the dance is about. For example, when ballet approaches the body as a machinery that can be developed to accomplish more or better, and energy is seen as something that helps to achieve these goals, then the body's facility at revealing its mastery is deemed a significant part of what the dance represents. When somatics, by contrast, conceptualizes the body as a sacrosanct individuality that must be protected and, equally, treats energy as something that is precious and must be meted out very carefully, then bodily identity develops from a capacity to move with ease, fluidity, and efficiency, and these become values that dancing itself produces and instantiates. Alternatively, contact improvisation constitutes the body as a dynamism engaging with other similar or dissimilar forces, so that the play of energy throughout the space becomes one of the central and defining products of the dance. This play of energy assumes the primary level of importance when determining what the dance is about.

As these three examples illustrate, dance's energy establishes and conveys meanings, and it also contributes to the definition of subjecthood for those involved in any given dance practice. Energy helps to construct the autonomous individualities of the ballet and somatics dancers, just as it facilitates the fusion of two bodies into a singular entity during contact improvisation. As the example of Pichet Klunchun considered at the beginning of this essay suggests, energy may also help to define the dancer's relationship to the world. It can, as Klunchun intimates, serve as the medium for a reciprocal exchange between dancer and surroundings or, alternatively, as the vehicle for asserting the singularity and independence of the dancer's vitality. Thus, focusing on energy as a central component of dancing yields insights about what dance communicates, and it also enables dancers and viewers to question what kinds of relationships they want to enter into with the body and the world.

Works Cited

George, Doran (2014): »A Conceit of the Natural Body: The Universal-Individual in Somatic Dance Training.« (PhD, University of California, Los Angeles).

Novack, Cynthia (1990): *Sharing the Dance: Contact Improvisation and American Culture*, (Madison, WI: University of Wisconsin Press).

Aesthetic Scenarios of *Energeia*
Bodies as Transformational Fields of Force

Sabine Huschka

> I am no more philosophical than my legs,
> but from them I sense this fact: that they
> are infused with energy that can be re-
> leased in movement (to appear to be
> motionless is its own kind of intoxicating
> movement) – that the shape the move-
> ment takes is beyond the fathoming of
> my mind's analysis but clear to my eyes
> and rich to my imagination.
> *(Merce Cunningham 1997: 86)*

Both an awareness and a discussion of energy(s) are blatantly present in professional dancing. Both significant and precarious, their practices and discourses indicate an awareness of the body's energetic states, address the sensation and design of the qualities of movement, and are oriented towards their performance. To have energies at one's disposal; to call them up; initiate them; circulate them; strengthen them; exhaust them; or simply allow them to *be* outlines a diverse and heterogeneous aesthetic field of work that is characteristically significant for professional dancing during the 20ᵗʰ century, as well as for contemporary dance. Within this process, aesthetic and choreographic approaches to movement address the body as a source of energy. They then extrapolate those force fields related to the transformative powers and transgressive competence of movement, in order to highlight the specific dimensions of this effect. The fundamental (physical) knowledge of energy, which – although without explicitly knowing »what energy *is*« (Feynman 1987: 60) – nonetheless ultimately manifests a process of change and transformation as evidence, finds its way into professional dance through the question of the body's transformational potential for movement. It instigates discussions about bodily and perception-based politics and the socio-cultural dispositions of the body, as well as about its scenic-theatrical functions. The implicit knowledge about energy manifests itself in somatic, movement-related and choreographic practices that model the body as agents of movement and present the energetic as an aesthetic force field of transgressions, which oscillate between utopia and critical intervention. Emerging as an aesthetic force field, the body becomes a thematically staged movement scenario of evoked energies.

Relevant analytical questions thus present themselves: How do movement and choreographic processes actually address energies and bring them forth as aesthetic forces? Which functions do they assume? And – to address the central question of this volume – what actually becomes visible in the energetic as an aesthetic force?

The Energetic Between Indefiniteness and a Concrete Orientation

Interestingly enough, contemporary artistic discourses on dance and performance have coalesced enough to agree to the terms of a specific energetic force in performances.[1] Dance critics describe a given choreography as »a work ... full of energy« (Amaya 29.08.2018) or attribute their »essence to an energy-sprinkling oscillation between the beautiful and the alienating, the comical and the tragic« (Riggert 31.5.2017). Any discussion of the energetic refers to a specific range of perception and effect, as outlined by a particularly transformational quality and experience. The energetic here indicates a qualitative moment of particular power, which according to Erika Fischer-Lichte's theatrical theorem of the *performative* enables the fundamental

---

1 Elena Philipp and Astrid Kaminski remark, for example: »We still work very much with visual axes and clear orientations in theatrical productions. In dance a space is loaded with atmospheric meaning: it is about energies and sensual impressions that are beyond the visual or acoustic.« (Philipp), »[Meg Stuart] is known for her high-energy pieces, in which performers embody different states of consciousness. Their often brutal longing for presence is contrasted with differing interior architectures between the stage, installation and ambience« (Kaminski). (Kaminski/Philipp 11.10.2018).

presentation of the theatre as an event space.[2] However, that discourse also lacks a qualitatively determinative differentiation – apart from the fundamental fact that an almost penetrating power of effect is closely connected to the energetic.[3] The striking use of the energetic as a single conceptual figure therefore does not clarify or resolve questions regarding its transformational qualities or design options. Instead, it remains undetermined what the energetic actually makes apparent, how it transmits and functions, and via which framings it could effectively become perceptible.

While discourses of energy in dance criticism indicate an increased qualitative horizon of experience, statements by contemporary choreographers open up an interesting range between certainty and an articulated domain of not-knowing, particularly regarding those specific qualities often referred to as ›energy‹ during the working process. Meg Stuart, for example, notes in an interview: »I am talking less about states than about energies. Does something have its own energy and, if so, how do I get access to it? How can we channel energy and bring it into a form? The body is not a piano!« (Stuart, in: Kaminski 21.06.2018). What she describes here is an approximation process that assigns any body dealing with energies its own *agency* beyond any specific instrumental use. In her intensive choreographic examination of ecstatic and intoxicated scenarios, Doris Uhlich also articulates a constitutive non-understanding of the energetic processes, to which her *Techno Trilogy* applies:

I watch the dancers. There is something I don't understand. I wonder why the concept of movement involved in eliminating borders thrills me so. The boom energy that gets discharged triggers something existential in me, both

---

2 In Erika Fischer-Lichte's theatrical theorem of the performative, discussions of the energetic function as an aesthetic conceptual figure. Originating in a transferring »source of energy«, this displays the fundamental presentation of the theatre as an event space. Fischer-Lichte writes: »They (the spectators) sense the power emanating from the actor, which forces them to focus their full attention on him without feeling overwhelmed and perceive it as a source of energy. The spectators sense that the actor is present in an unusually intense way, granting them in turn an intense sensation of themselves as present. To them, presence occurs as an intense experience of ›presentness‹« (Fischer-Lichte 2008: 96).

3 If one was to apply Hans-Thies Lehmann's work, a discussion of ›energy‹ could initiate a theoretical work striving for a »conceptual recording and verbalization of experience« (Lehmann 1999: 16).

when I am watching and when I am dancing it. That's what I'm trying to pin down. (Uhlich 2016)

Boris Charmatz thematizes *energy* in the context of an impending exhaustion, with which dancers have to deal in light of their extremely high physical demands. As such, any energetic expenditure outside of a performance seems to be coated in a haze of ›worthlessness‹, since it fails to create a valuable trace beyond the performance event.[4] As he writes: »however, I do not let this inhibit my taste for a highly demanding, energetic form of dance, to only privilege, instead, an immobile, slow, floor-based form. I thrive on the state of tension and contrasts and high levels of physical and mental concentration« (Charmatz 2011: 131). Charmatz thus assigns energy to an almost imperative process of expenditure in dance, which he tries to present as a »discipline of effort«.[5] Interestingly enough, the aesthetic examination of energy in the work of all three choreographers represents a socio-political criticism of our exhaustion as caused by the world we live in and its constant striving for efficiency.

In fact, contemporary dance performances reflect thematically striking and concise choreographic elaborations of energy.[6] For example: in *Violet* (2011) by Meg Stuart/Damaged Goods, energy processes scenarios charged with stress into movement »in reaction to states of exhaustion [... and] energy patterns of nature« (Stuart 2018:11).[7] *Pieces and Elements* (2016) by Isabelle

---

4 »This relationship to energy expenditure is a fundamental aspect for dance. There is an almost metaphysical dimension, something totally gratuitous about this ›worthless‹ expenditure that neither ›counts‹ nor ›calculate[s]‹« (Charmatz 2011: 132).

5 »There is a fine line between the idea of performing movement ›at a loss‹ and a ›discipline of effort‹« (Ibid: 132). In terms of the extent to which Charmatz conceived of his own danced art as anti-capitalist, in terms of his perspectivation on dancing as a process of energetic expenditure, see Lucia Ruprecht's chapter: *Gesture, Energy, Critique: Robert Longo and Boris Charmatz* in this volume.

6 To name only a few recent pieces, these include: Doris Uhlich's *The Techno-Trilogy* (2014-2016); Margrét Sara Guðjónsdóttir *Conspiracy Ceremony* (2017) and *Pervasive Magnetic Stimuli* (2018); Kat Válastur's *Rasp Your Soul* (2017) Dance Company Rubato's *Flirren* (2017); Isabelle Schad's *Turning Solo* (2017); Wilhelm Groener's *Schleppen* (2017); Liz Rosenfeld *If You Ask Me What I Want, I'll Tell You, I Want Everything* (2017); and Batsheva Dance Company's *Venezuela* (2017).

7 »Violet‹ (2011) is a completely abstract piece about the energy patterns in nature. In it, five dancers interact with the five Platonic bodies. The piece was created around the time of the Arab Spring and the Tsunami in Japan, and during time I asked myself: What leads to

Schad addresses »the energetic potential of bodies, in order to question the modes of being together: as body, self and group« (Schad 2016). In their piece *Schleppen* (2017) Wilhelm Groener also deal with these fields of forces that »affect the body, but also those which emanate from it« (Groener 2017).[8] Doris Uhlich's *Techno-Trilogy* presents aesthetic figurations of intoxication in order to »flood the theatre space with energy« and »transfer energies« (Uhlich 2017). Finally, in *Pervasive Magnetic Stimuli* (2018), Margrét Sara Guðjónsdóttir sets out to »explore forces that surround and fulfill us all [...] through a language of endless presence that simultaneously reveals and penetrates its surroundings« (Guðjónsdóttir 2018).

According to the Greek root of the word »energeia«, »effective forces« can actually be found at work by means of intensity-charged body states and movements. In this sense, and in what can therefore be described as aesthetic scenarios of *energeia*, the energetic is directed towards a scenic event that ›invokes‹, generates, and even seeks to play forces off against one another. In many of these productions, this work with the energetic makes the desire to transgress and traverse borders apparent. The extent to which this downright transgressive striving is met with an aesthetic work on the border, which itself seeks to traverse borders oscillating between aesthetic intervention and the longing for utopias, is illustrated by the following analyses, particularly in terms of individual scenes.

---

change? When will there be a radical rethink and how will we deal with it? Actually it was the reaction to a state of exhaustion: I do not have the strength for all this ... Normally you have all the time in the world for abstraction, because it is a cold and distant concept. You work with lines, forces, geometries ... But here we worked with abstract movements under stress, during a charged, even »hot« time. There was an urgency, an assignment. That's why I had the feeling that it was very political« (Stuart 2018: 11).

8 »In this work, both the forces acting on the body and also those emanating from it transform the body into an area of friction and a space of resonance, as well as a representative of multiple projections. [...] What adheres to and within us, what slows, what attracts us, what makes us resilient« (Wilhelm Groener 2017).

Energeia as an Aesthetic Force Field:
Aspects of its Political Dimensions

Interestingly, when considering the question »Why is there always energy for dancing?« Susan Foster argues for an experiential exposure of energies in dancing. These could refill the body from an undreamt-of surplus reservoir of power, and push its capacity even beyond the line of exhaustion. As she explains: »[D]ancing ... produces the energy to sustain itself as an activity« (Foster 2016: 12). On the basis of this observation, Foster sets herself in conversation with various theoretical approaches (Johan Huizinga, Jean Piaget, Sondra Fraleigh, Susanne Langer and Randy Martin), ultimately leading to the question: when »dance arouses or contributes to a sense of abundant energy, what explanations have been put forward to account for this capacity?« (Foster 2016: 13). She thus emphasizes dance's often-underestimated cultural-social value: namely to open up a physical practice of interactive exchange and activation. This extends beyond the economic exchange of goods in neoliberal economic logic, and cultivates the physical practice of plurality and social gathering. The socio-cultural potential of dance becomes recognizable due to and precisely because of this physical mobilization practice, which creates and sharpens an awareness of energy as processes of social interaction. In summary, Foster stresses:

> By locating dance's energy as a sign of plenty, even abundance, and not as a means [for] accomplishing some other objective – [...] – we are able to contemplate a kind of richness that we are often encouraged to ignore. Indeed, dance may provide an exceptional example of just how generous people are and how willing they might be to enter into a more general dance of the social. (Foster 2016: 23)

In terms of culture and society, dance therefore reflects energy's fundamental potential to open up physical ways of creation, forms of action, and options for transformation. These are created in such a way that energy can become understandable and realized as an inexhaustible process of exchange, as well as a space for social action.

André Lepecki develops a comparably optimistic cultural perspective on dance as »*Engaged Action*« (Lepecki 2013: 30), and emphasizes the conceptual figure of *energeia* as the fundamental political potential of dance. Introduced as a constitutive element of the political, *energeia* in the sense of an Aristotelian figure of thought contains a dimension that qualifies movement:

> As *work* that works, as *energy* that energizes, and as *movement* that in moving triggers action, the semantic field defined by *energeia* is one without which there would be no politics; and indeed, no dancing. *Energeia* qualifies movement (*kinesis*) not only as something that moves, but as a motion that *acts*. It is thanks to it that a movement becomes activation and actualization – of corporeal and critical capacities towards the composition and formation of engaged modes of existence. (Ibid.)

This essay cannot offer a detailed presentation or analysis of Lepecki's complex philosophical examination of the perceptual political positions between engagement and dis-engagement in dance art. However, in short, for Lepecki *energeia* marks an »affective-energetic field necessary for the concrete initiation and actualization of any movement that acts because engaged with a specific political situation and its demands.« (Ibid.: 31) The concept of *energeia* thus refers to the philosophical relevance of meaning: as an affective-energetic structure, *energeia* constructs a space for the initiation and activation of movement, which articulates itself as a political context for action. Lepecki explains the relationship between *energeia* and a politicizing action structure of movement – or as its articulated political stance in motion – through *energeia's* inner structure and its eventful initiation as a movement. Lepecki stresses that *energia* is always accompanied by a »profoundly political and kinetic phenomenon« (ibid.: 32), as Hannah Arendt's political theory clarifies. Identified with an initiating moment or, more precisely, with an initiating factor of and in motion, *energeia* identifies itself as a physical and perceptual political disposition of engagement as action.

If one considers the concrete movement and aesthetic oriented procedures of the art of dance – especially in terms of their many diverse elaborate references and approaches to the energetic, as well as their conceptual and discursive figures of energy – it becomes clear that what constitutes the core of their aesthetic work is actually a moment of initiation in the sense of an activation of movement forces. This investigation of energy ought to lead the body into specific power structures, from which the body begins to experience itself as moving its own self toward the realization of movement.

These power structures could be somatically guided, for example, via conscious breathing, muscle-relaxation, or imaginative exercises. The respective cognitive and political arrangement between body and energy is rooted in an involvement (engagement) in activation processes. These originate out of energetic processes' specific motives and orientations for and of initiating movement. The embodied-mental and imaginative processes of negotiation with energies, in turn, therefore call into question the initiating-activating moments and factors in and for a movement itself. The ways in which a movement is initiated must also negotiate bodily conceptions as an aesthetic force, with which contrary conceivable-political dispositions of *agency* become concrete.

Primarily applied here is an aesthetic work that makes the body thematic as an organum, carrier, instrument or medium of movement. That is to say: the performative and quite idiosyncratic potentiality of the body to be able to mobilize and thereby initiate forces becomes an aesthetic force, in the sense of a consciously designed access to energy. Therefore *energeia*, in the Aristotelian sense as an »always already realized possibility« (Liske 1991: 172),[9] becomes the aesthetic venue for the negotiation of movement.

In concrete terms, these applied processes – which are permeated by physiological knowledge, and imaginative and perception-guiding processes – seek to release, accentuate, liquefy, accelerate or regulate movements to form aesthetic physical models with divergent political strategies. Susan Foster expands upon this in her chapter *Dancing the Energy/Energizing the Dancing* in terms of ballet, somatics and contact improvisation. Energetically operating training methods such as Gaga, with their approaches to instinctive and libidinal energy and force fields, are especially explicit in demonstrating a body politic of transgression. This promotes and demands mental and physical flexibility, as well as an innovative willingness to move between controlled expression and enhanced pleasure. The body's transformational competence means that dancers must train to be ›gifted‹ in the act of constant transformation itself. By fitting themselves into the economies of a neoliberal dance market, these dancers will come to measure

---

9 As Liske distinctly analyzes it, *energeia* according to Aristotle indicates a »pure realization« in which »no remnant remains of any yet to be realized possibility.« (Liske 1991: 172) *Energeia* is therefore: »The realization of an ... already formed or just completed capacity ... which in turn is a completed realization, to the extent that such an activity represents a goal (in itself), so that in the exercise itself its conclusion is already reached« (Liske 1991: 173).

their own personal and calculable capital in the future. This is namely – as Meghan Quinlan emphasizes in her contribution to this volume – to be physically, emotionally and mentally flexible and innovative.

Every bodily-aesthetic form of work in professional dancing demands that the body mobilizes forces in order to initiate movements. But aesthetic work with *energeia* is explicitly aimed at initiating the process of moving-oneself. This is directed towards the body's own transformational and transforming movement-competence, which strives for *and* demands its own transgression. The performative and thoroughly idiosyncratic potential of the body to be able to mobilize itself leads to a process of negotiation with the momentum of initiation, which hands responsibility for the body over to an aesthetic force field and transcends it as the subject of »its own movements«.[10] This is the aesthetic work on *energeia*: the initiation of aesthetic fields of force that apply to the transgressions of the body (via its abilities, its possibilities, its images and its concepts).[11] A practice thus becomes qualified in which the body's gift of moving itself notably emerges as an aesthetic structure that consciously invades, infects and confronts the body as it moves.

Transgressions: Working on the Border

Transgression carries the limit right to the limit of its being; transgression forces the limit to face the fact of its imminent disappearance, to find itself in what it excludes (perhaps, to be more exact, to recognize itself for the first time), to experience its positive truth in its downward fall? [...] Transgression, then, is not related to the limit as black to white, the prohibited to the lawful, the outside to the inside, or as the open area of a building to its enclosed

---

10 See Lehmann (pp. 84-85) and his explanations of transgression: »which indicate a moment of excess and immanent self-endangerment, a turn of the subject against himself.« Even while Lehmann depicts »the core of the tragic experience« in transgression, his figure of thought also clarifies the decisive paradox of the aesthetic work on energy, namely: »that even the self›itself is [...] constituted by nothing other than its loss.«

11 Beyond a capacity which, according to Christoph Menke, is »a socially predetermined general form [...] oriented towards success« (Menke 2013: 13), aesthetic forces are suited to the effect of transformations. They bring forth something »that is beyond what they have always been« (Ibid.).

spaces. Rather, their relationship takes the form of a spiral which no simple infraction can exhaust. *(Foucault 1977: 34-35)*[12]

The choreographic works of the Austrian performer and choreographer Doris Uhlich, for example, illustrate how initiation forms and scenarios of movement call for an examination of one's own and other's causes of movement, while also exposing the body as moving itself – in the same instant of its own activation – toward an activation. Between re-, de- and activation processes, Uhlich's movement scenarios negotiate a choreographic structure of moving oneself by becoming moved, which unfolds itself as a game played between one's own and foreign forces.

In her solo piece *Universal Dancer*, the first part of her *Techno-Trilogy*, a vibrating machine materializes a force field of being moved in moving oneself. The centre of the stage is dominated by a wooden platform, and a motor mounted on the underside makes the lower part of this construction shake. Uhlich uses this contraption as an example of force, so as to theatrically unfold scenes depicting the human body exposed to and in conflict with the force field of a foreign body. Uhlich stands, sits, or lays upon this platform, and allows the vibrations to spread throughout her body. These physical reverberations effectively allow a foreign force to perpetuate itself in her own body, for she has yielded to the impulse of its movements. Uhlich allows her flesh to shudder, shake and vibrate as her muscles relax. In doing so, she allows her own ability to move to be carried away by the machine, as it draws her into its own kinetic-kinaesthetic vibrational field. As her body trembles, the mechanical power of the vibrating machine amalgamates into a situation of the almost »medialized-materialized« (»mediation« or »mediatization«) transmission of energies, in which the body moves. The awkward influence of foreign forces is also presented, which organically asserts itself over the body while also conceding responsibility for it. Consequently, a transformation of Uhlich's movement-body occurs. Out of this complex interdependence of simultaneously becoming moved inside of one's own act of moving,

---

12 Although Foucault's »Preface to Transgression«, written in homage to Georges Bataille, is devoted to reflections on the emergence of sexuality, his philosophical thoughts allow for reflections upon space of the energetic as an aesthetic intervention of transgression. See also Neumann 2003.

a transgressive force is enacted, which presents the aesthetic power of the body in its radically changeable and transformative structure.[13]

Figure 1: Doris Uhlich in *Universal Dancer* (2014). Choreographed by Doris Uhlich.

In this piece, Uhlich points out energy's movement-aesthetic negotiation processes, which reveal themselves as an aesthetic bodily scenario via the echo of foreign movements in one's own movement of oneself. Within this process, the body experiences itself as a subjected and self-controlled instance of movement as a boundary, for it is exposed to the foreign forces of being moved even in its own moving of itself. These foreign initiating power structures both transcend the body and simultaneously oppose its act by the desire to transgress and transverse borders. What becomes apparent here is the aesthetic scenario of *energeia*, which refers to a basic feature of its aesthetic power in the space of the body: namely the realization of transgression as aesthetic work on this border.

The extent to which choreographers' aesthetic interest of energy exceeds their knowledge and their desire for delimitation can also be observed in Cunningham's choreographic method, which takes an aleatoric approach

---

13 See also Huschka 2018.

when arranging movement. In order to use movement to release the energy penetrating the body, as Cunningham has always emphasized,[14] and in order to explore increasing possibilities of the physical forms of movement, he designs movements by means of a randomly guided construction process. In being so far removed from his own body, the written draft of randomly constructed movement patterns provokes a radical aesthetic work at the limits of physical possibilities. In dealing with abstract movement constructs, the dancers' (admittedly quite radical) work of constantly transgressing themselves is intended to realize their own embodied ability to move in this way.[15] For Cunningham, this choreographic process represents an aesthetic work on energies: energy can only emerge through a conscious detachment from one's own body, as the body is transgressed and pulled out of its emotional-expressive structures. The aleatoric method provokes the foreign situation of moving oneself, which opens up energy as an aesthetic power.

The degree to which an aesthetic work on energy as an initial transformative process seeks to transgress the dancing's body's ability to transcend its own borders strikingly characterizes aesthetic strategies of contemporary dance until today. As Foucault explains: »Transgression opens onto a scintillating and constantly affirmed world, a world without shadow or twilight, without that serpentine ›no‹ that bites into fruits and lodges their contradictions at their core.« (Foucault 1977: 37) Statements by contemporary choreographers such as Meg Stuart explicitly applies the utopian figure of transgression that Foucault develops as a conceptual figure of boundaries: »I believe that we all want to escape our everyday reality. We want to have the feeling that we are merging with something else [...] that the borders between us and others can be overcome« (Stuart 2018: 9). Implied in this statement is the knowledge that transgression »is to measure the excessive distance that it opens at the heart of the limit and to trace the flashing line that causes the limit to arise« (Foucault 1997: 35).

---

14   See the opening quote in this chapter: (Cunningham 1997: 86).
15   See also Huschka 2000.

Figure 2: Suet-Wan Tsang in *Pervasive Magnetic Stimuli* (2018).
Choreographed by Margrét Sara Guðjónsdóttir.

According to physics, *energeia* occurs as a transformation without consuming itself or being produced. Dance seems to want to add an aesthetic reverberation to this knowledge, due to the socially rampant states of exhaustion existentially affecting dancers. Interestingly, it is therefore the physical states of *exhaustion* that, in the works of Icelandic choreographer Margrét Sara Guðjónsdóttir, become the occasion for aesthetic research into *energizing* states. Guðjónsdóttir emphasizes in a personal interview that these states, emerging from the body's exhaustion, unleash intensive release and relaxation, and thus allow »other forces« to ascend. The dancers' trance-filled bodies reveal themselves to the audience in long-lasting (and outwardly seemingly stationary) states of affective turbulence, which offer a glimpse into the absence of representation lingering behind their heavy eyelids [see Fig. 2]. The sensory-affective force structure of their agitated fields of forces persevere in particular, long-lasting moments, which expose the initiation of visible forms of energy in states of transformative power. This choreographic work operates at the limit of visibility, in order to demand a certain perceptual work from the audience, who are called upon to expose themselves to the sensitively disturbing moment of the energetic as an aesthetic space.

Works Cited

Charmatz, Boris (2011): »Energy.« In: Boris Charmatz/Isabelle Launay (eds.): *Undertraining. On A Contemporary Dance* (Musée de la danse – Centre chorégraphique national de Rennes et de Bretagne: Les presses du réel), pp. 131-132.

Cunningham, Merce (1997): »The Impermanent Art (1952).« In: David Vaughan: *Merce Cunnigham Fifty Years. Chronicle and Commentary by David Vaughan,* (New York: Aperture Books), pp. 86-87.

Feynman, Richard P. (1987): *Vorlesung über Physik, Bd. 1. Hauptsächlich Mechanik, Strahluug und Wärme,* (München/Wien: Oldenbourg Wissenschaftsverlag), cited in Christian Kassung (2013): »Was bleibt und was nicht bleibt. Eine sehr kurze Geschichte der Energie.« In: Barbara Gronau (ed.): *Szenarien der Energie. Zur Ästhetik und Wissenschaft des Immatriellen,* (Bielefeld: transcript), pp. 15-23.

Fischer-Lichte, Erika (2008 [2004]): *The Transformative Power of Performance. A New Aesthetics,* (London/New York: Routledge).

Foster, Susan (2016): »Why Is There Always Energy for Dancing?« In: *Dance Research Journal,* (48/3), pp. 11-26.

Foucault, Michel (2000): »Vorrede zur Überschreitung.« In: Michel Foucault: *Von der Subversion des Wissens,* (Frankfurt a. M: Fischer Taschenbuch Verlag), pp. 28-45.

Foucault, Michel (1977): »A Preface to Transgression.« In: Donald F. Bouchard (ed. and trans.): *Michel Foucault. Language, Counter-Memory, Practice. Selected Essays and Interviews,* (Ithaca/New York: Cornell University Press), pp. 29-52.

Huschka, Sabine (2010): »Merce Cunningham: Der Tanz als Ort Sich-Anders zu machen.« In: Friederike Lampert (ed.): *Choreographieren reflektieren,* (Münster: LIT-Verlag), pp. 157-166.

Huschka, Sabine (2013): »Low Energy – High Energy: Motive der Energetisierung von Körper und Publikum im Tanz.« In: Barbara Gronau (ed.): *Szenarien der Energie,* (Bielefeld: transcript), pp. 201-222.

Huschka, Sabine (2018): »Tanzästhetische Strategien von Rausch: Körper/ Szenen der Ausschreitung.« In: Olivia Ebert/Eva Holling/Nikolaus Müller-Schöll/Philipp Schulte, Bernhard Siebert/Gerald Siegmund (eds.): *Theater als Kritik.* (Bielefeld: transcript), pp. 261-271.

Lepecki, André (2013): »From Partaking to Initiating. Leadingfollowing as Dance's (a-personal) Political Singularity.« In: Gerald Siegmund/Stefan Hölscher (eds.): *Dance, Politics & Co-Immunity*, (Zürich: Diaphanes), pp. 21-38.

Liske, Michael-Thomas (1991): »Kinesis und Energeia bei Aristoteles.« In: *Phronesis* 36/2, pp. 161-178.

Neumann, Gerhard/Warning, Rainer (eds.) (2003): *Transgressionen: Literatur als Ethnographie*, (Freiburg i.br.: Rombach).

Lehmann, Hans-Thies (1999): *Postdramatisches Theater*, (Frankfurt a.M.: Verlag der Autoren).

Online Sources

Amaya, Sasha (29.08.2018): »The Sound of Energy. In correspondence with Lina Gómez.« www.tanzraumberlin.de/Artist-Profile-Lina-Gomez--230 4-0.html [Accessed 6.12.2018]

Guðjónsdóttir, Margrét Sara: »*Pervasive Magnetic Stimuli*.« Premiere 01.11.2018, Sophiensaele Berlin. http://msgudjonsdottir.com/pervasive-magnetic-st imuli/1788 [Accessed 14.12.2018]

Kaminski, Astrid und Philipp, Elena (11.10.2018): »Tanz und Sprechtheater – Ein Gespräch über die Verflechtung der Künste. Betriebsunfall einer Beziehung.« *Nachtkritik*. https://nachtkritik.de/index.php?option=com_co ntent&view=article&id=15936:tanz-und-sprechtheater-ein-gespraech -ueber-die-verflechtung-der-kuenste&catid=101& Itemid=84 [Accessed 5.12.2018]

Kaminski, Astrid (21.06.2018): »Choreografin Stuart über Stuart: ›Der Körper ist kein Klavier‹. Anlass für ein Gespräch über Transformation.« *taz*. www.taz.de/!5514264/ [Accessed 09.12.2018]

Riggert, Charlotte (31.5.2017): »Das Pferd der Geschichte«, »Groteske Tennisspieler*innen lotsen uns quer durch die Kulturgeschichte: ›Jaguar‹ von Marlene Monteiro Freitas in Zusammenarbeit mit Andreas Merk im HAU 2.« *Tanzraumberlin*. www.tanzraumberlin.de/Jaguar--1821-0.html [Accessed 6.12.2018]

Schad, Isabelle (2016): »Pieces and Elements.« Programmankündigung Premiere 27.11.2016 am HAU Hebbel am Ufer Berlin. www.tanzforumberlin. de/produktion/pieces-and-elements/ [Accessed 6.12.2018]

Stuart, Meg (2018): in »Erschöpfung als Strategie. Hans Ulrich Obrist im Gespräch mit der Choreografin Meg Stuart über Rituale, Improvisation und Ekstase.« *Anderer Zustand, Das Magazin #30*, edited by Kulturstiftung des Bundes Halle an der Saale, Potsdam, pp. 8-11. https://www.kulturstiftung-des-bundes.de/de/magazin/magazin_30/erschoepfung_als_strategie.html [Accessed 5.12.2018]

Uhlich, Doris (2016): »Boom Bodies.« http://dorisuhlich.at/en/projects/31-boom-bodies [Accessed 5.12.2018]

Uhlich, Doris (2017): »Universal Dancer.« www.dorisuhlich.at/de/projekte/4-universal-dancer [Accessed: 09.12.2018]

Wilhelm Groener (2017): »Schleppen.« Programmankündigung. Premiere 01.11.2017 Tanzfabrik Berlin; www.tanzforumberlin.de/produktion/schleppen/ [Accessed 5.12.2018]

»I was seeking and finally discovered the central spring of all movement«[1]
Configurations of Energy Discourses in Dancers' Autobiographies

Christina Thurner

In her 1927 autobiography *My Life*, Isadora Duncan explains: »My ideas on dance were to express the feelings and emotions of humanity.« (1927: 36) The idea of dance as an expression of human feelings and emotions may initially appear to be obvious. However, upon closer examination the question of how these feelings and sensations are expressed through dance becomes more relevant to the scholarly study of dance. This raises the further question of how these perceptions could in turn become a specific type of dance within the history of dance itself, as interpreted historiographically. Duncan loads this interpretation »with an existential experience«, in which dancers become aware of an »energetic principle of their own bodies« (Huschka 2000: 53).[2] The danced expression of these sensations is thus associated with the energetic principle of the body in the historiography of dance. But how does historiography come to discourse configurations of the energetic, on the basis of statements on danced expression? These configurations are of particular interest, because a dance itself no longer ›exists‹ at the time of writing. That historians might otherwise rely on pictures, photographs, or some filmed footage for their study is nonetheless another issue, as this article is exclusively concerned with descriptions of dance as it is physically performed.

---

1 Duncan 1927, p. 75.

2 Translator's note: The original quote reads: »in der sie […] ein […] energetisches Prinzip ihres Körpers gewahr […]«.

The configurations described in this article are understood to mean dynamic fields of discourse, interdependent networks of expression, narrations, as well as phenomena.[3] Relying on the example of Duncan and other exponents of the 20th century history of dance, this article will examine the relationship between dance historical discourses and autobiographical testimonies, in respect to the specific representations of energetic forces in dance. I will focus on so-called self-expressions, precisely because the energetic affects the (subjective) level of experience. And because this work is about historical experiences, I will rely upon what has been written, that is to say on auto-bio-graphies. In so doing, I will focus my attention upon a genre of sources that has previously been neglected or at least uncritically used by dance-theory, and which I will investigate epistemologically so as to create an exemplary productive example.[4]

For example, the connection between forces and sentiments in Duncan's memoirs can be read in this manner. She understands her ›dance studies‹ (1928: 76) firstly as an inwardly-focused and then as an externally-mediated controlled energetic practice, (which shall be discussed in greater detail short-ly), as Balanchine's ballerina Toni Bentley explains in her *Dancer's Journal*: »All our physical energy is the overflow of spiritual feelings« (2003: 16). This statement encompasses physical energy as something that erupts or pours forth from the body. In light of these arguments, the question arises for scholars of dance as to how they might address such self-expressions by dancers regarding their energetic experiences. How can »the energetic« be transformed into discourse? How can it be described in terms of (varying) understandings and phenomena of dance? Which conclusions can be gen-erated from such statements with regards to the scholarly examination of physical forces? And how? These questions will be addressed below. First, however, a short reflection upon the nature of the source text will be offered.

---

3 This could be compared, amongst others, to Keller 2011, p. 239, Regarding the concept of the figuration, see also: Brandl-Risi/Ernst/Wagner 2000; Boehm/Brandstetter/von Müller 2007.

4 See also the research platform I initiated at the University of Bern: www.wbkolleg.unibe. ch/research/research_forum/auto_bio_graphy__historiographic_perspectives_on_ego_ documents_personal_testimonies_in_literature_and_the_visual_and_performative_ arts/index_eng.html, (August 14, 2018).

Consultation of literary studies of autobiographies can allow one to ascertain helpful methodological tools with which to approach these texts. Yet philological and dance-specific approaches also differ fundamentally in some respects, especially concerning epistemological interest, and as regards the ›object‹ and therefore the focus. For this dance-studies research on autobiographies, it is also important to recognize the existing wide range of definitions, which I here condense into the following: I agree with Michaela Holdenried's argument that autobiography »can not be more closely defined than by an elucidation of what the expression actually means: the description (*graphia*) of the life (*bios*) of an individual as told by themselves (*auto*)« (2000: 21).[5]

This definition, which is so closely related to the compound itself, is meaningful in its emphasis of three central aspects: 1) the process of writing (as something dynamic); 2) the focus on a life; that is to say on 3) one's own (subjectively perceived) life. I argue that the most important features are therefore determined, which should always be reflected in the analysis of this text or in relation to the function of these sources. Moreover, the literary scholar and autobiography researcher Martina Wagner-Egelhaaf explains that the functions of author, narrator and protagonist merge in the retrospective recounting of an autobiography (2005: 6). As critical readers we must continuously remain aware that each autobiography contains a retroactive reconstruction of the self as a unified identity. This construction and its particular mechanisms must always be taken into account in any subsequent analysis. Such mechanisms are revealed in the justifications for why and how that particular autobiography was written, for example the author's gesture. Like many other autobiographers, for example using the field of dance, the Russian ballerina Maija Plissezkaja wants to tell her life truthfully, even »to help the truth [...] to be true [...]« (2006 [1994]: 9). This attitude can also be understood in a political context. Nevertheless, it is interesting that Duncan already relativizes such a claim by asking herself: »How can we write the truth about ourselves? Do we even know it?« (1927: 1).[6] The so-called »truth« is therefore more or less reflectively declared to be the claim of autobiographical writing.

To briefly summarize: such an authorial gesture, as well as the explicit ›subjectivity‹ of these sources, both demand their own historiographical

---

5 Holdenried makes implicit reference here to Misch.

6 See also Ibid, p. 3.

procedures. These then, however, allow dance history to be rewritten, especially with regard to energetic forces and movements of expression. In other words: autobiographies cannot simply explain anything ›authentically‹. Rather, they must be read, contextualized, and interpreted in a certain way, so that they can in turn allow for particular dance-historical expressions.

This will be demonstrated in the following three steps. On the basis of dancer autobiographies, I will examine the example of the relationship between discourse figurations of the energetic, and then the scholarly insights about dance that can be drawn from them. This will be done firstly, regarding the aspect of *receiving energies, i.e. activating and mobilizing forces*; secondly from the perspective of *energetic practice, i.e. regulating and directing forces*; and thirdly regarding *energy consumption, the experience of exhaustion of forces*.

Receiving Energies (Activating and Mobilizing Forces)

In Martha Graham's autobiography *Blood Memory*, which was published in English in 1991, (the year of her passing at age 97), we find her retrospective look at her long dancer's life:

> I have based everything that I have done on the pulsation of life, which is, to me, the pulsation of breath. Every time you breathe life in or expel it, it is a release or a contraction. It is that basic to the body. You are born with these two movements and you keep both until you die. But you begin to use them consciously so that they are beneficial to dance dramatically. You must animate that energy within yourself. (Graham 1991: 46)

This retrospective statement is remarkable in that it comes from a dancer, choreographer and dance teacher who – as she was aware – had developed, established and passed on a highly successful dance aesthetic. This, in turn, is based on a specific technique that is still closely connected to Graham's work today, and which has been described both by herself and in adjacent research on energetic impulses as contraction and release.[7] It is interesting that she presents this technique, here and in other parts of her autobiogra-

---

7 On this topic see also Huschka 2002, p. 216ff.

phy, as a quasi anthropological process using the image of animation. She even goes so far as to compare the energy used in dance with a driving force[8] that – according to her – »sustains the world and the universe. It animates the world and everything in it«. Graham continues: »I recognized early in my life that there was this kind of energy, some animating spark, or whatever you choose to call it« (1991: 46). This discursively presented figuration of the invigorating energetic spark initially seems to contradict the absolute discipline that Graham demands, with regard to her idea of dance.[9] However, she also writes that energy must be consciously activated and used in order to have a dramaturgical effect. She thus legitimizes – one could even conclude – her strict dance training with a discourse that justifies it vitalistically, or even cosmologically, and which connects it to an anthropological narrative.

If one establishes a reference to Duncan's discourse configuration, which at first glance seemingly corresponds, quite distinct ideas about dance soon become recognizable. Duncan also writes – 64 years before Graham – of a power awakening within: »do you not feel an inner self awakening deep within you – that it is by its strength that your head is lifted, that your arms are raised, that you are walking slowly toward the light?« (1927: 76) And she goes on to say that this awakening, the liberation of the inner emotion is, in her opinion, the beginning of all danced art (Duncan 1928: 77).[10] Let us take a closer look at how this mobilization of forces is described. While Graham experiences her bodily energy as an impulse, or as an invigorating spark analogous to the breath and the pulsating rhythm of life, Duncan first ›listens into‹ her inner self extensively. She then locates the particular place in the centre of her body (»the solar plexus«) (1927: 75) where the force is localized and originates, and from whence it can then expand and mediate. Duncan claims to have long sought and researched »the central spring of all movement«, which is »the crater of motor power, the unity from which all diversions of movements are born« (1927: 75).[11]

---

8 See also Graham 1992, p. 50.

9 For instance, see also Huschka 2002, p. 225.

10 See also Duncan 1927, p. 76: »This awakening is the first step in the dance, as I conceive it.«

11 The full passage reads: »I spent long days and nights in the studio seeking that dance which might be the divine expression of the human spirit through the medium of the body's movement. For hours I would stand quite still, my two hands folded between my breasts, covering the solar plexus. My mother often became alarmed to see me remain for such long intervals quite motionless as if in a trance – but I was seeking and finally discovered

Here, the autobiographer traces her way of dancing back to an intensive and enduring retreat into the body. She describes this as a practice that wants to be exercised. In fact, today we know of various practices that allow themselves to be similarly performed and verbalized. However, I am particularly interested in the historical view of this subjective and singularly constituent description, which makes it possible to understand this phenomenon of dance history in what I believe to be an epistemologically productive way. Duncan further explains that it was not until many months later, when she had learned to concentrate, that she discovered »that the vibrations of music« were »pouring into her like as if a light source« (1928: 76f). She concludes: »there they reflected themselves in Spiritual Vision not the brain's mirror, but the soul's, and from this vision I could express them in Dance« (Duncan 1927: 75).[12] Duncan presents the process of mobilizing forces as a specific skill, according to which she allows influences from outside – for example, the music in the quotation – to take effect in such a way that a particular expression emerges from this sensation.

Duncan also decisively contrasts this specifically crafted expression against imitations when she writes:

> At that Villa in Abbazia there was a palm tree before our windows. It was the first time I had seen a palm tree growing in a temperate climate. I used to notice its leaves trembling in the early morning breeze, and from them I created in my dance that light fluttering of the arms, hands and fingers, which has been so much abused by my imitators; for they forget to go to the original source and contemplate the movements of the palm tree, to receive them inwardly before giving them outwardly. (Duncan 1927: 109f)

According to Duncan, that which is perceived must first be processed internally, contemplatively, and energetically, and then translated into expression in order to have any effect.

---

the central spring of all movement, the crater of motor power, the unity from which all diversions of movements are born, the mirror of vision for the creation of the dance.«

12 The full passage reads: »After many months, when I had learned to concentrate all my force to this one fount of light within me—there they reflected themselves in Spiritual Vision not the brain's mirror, but the soul's, and from this vision I could express them in Dance.«

Energetic Practice (Regulation and Control of Forces)

Duncan establishes an instance here that – following long practice and a precise knowledge of its own inner power relations – absorbs external energies, processes them and conveys them to the outside world as dance. This becomes particularly clear in the following passage, in which she describes her collaboration with the conductor Walter Damrosch in the USA: »The mighty reverberation« of the orchestra has filled her inner self and – according to Duncan:

> I become the Medium to condense in unified expression the joy of Brünnhilde awakened by Siegfried, or the soul of Isolde seeking in Death her realization. Voluminous, vast, swelling like sails in the wind, the movement of my dance carry me onward–onward and upward, and I feel the presence of a mighty power within me which listens to the music and then reaches out through all my body, trying to find an outlet for this listening. Sometimes this power grew furious, sometimes it raged and shook me until my heart nearly burst from its passion, and I thought my last moments on earth had surely arrived. At other times it brooded heavily, and I would suddenly feel such anguish that, through my arms stretched to the Heavens, I implored help from where no help came. Often I thought to myself, what a mistake to call me a dancer–I am the magnetic centre to convey the emotional expressions of the Orchestra. From my soul sprang fiery rays to connect me with my trembling, vibrating Orchestra. (Duncan 1927: 223f)

In this passage, Duncan seeks to explain her energetic practice, and to interpret her own role therein by designating herself as a medium and a magnetic center. Duncan not only reflects the control of forces via dance on stage or through discourse in her memories; she also develops – as she puts it – »the theory on which I founded my school.« (Duncan 1927: 75) Duncan's initial comment on her theory is that, at first glance, a literal explanation seems extraordinarily difficult (1927:76).[13] However, the autobiographer also presents this mediation as a control of energies when she writes:

---

13 She writes: »It would seem as if it were a very difficult thing to explain in words«. See also: 1928, p. 77.

My powers of teaching seemed indeed to border on the marvelous. I had only
to hold out my hands towards the children and they danced. It was not even
as though I taught them to dance, but rather as if I opened a way by which the
Spirit of Dance flowed over them. (Duncan 1927: 304)

Such passages provide information about Duncan's understanding of dance,
of the generation of dance, of the way it is mediated, and of its intended perception. It is important here to emphasize that Duncan's autobiography also
contains other passages that relativize the »spirit of dance« (2016: 265), as
well as the discovery of »original movements« (1928: 78)[14] etc. Yet academic
research has seldom taken this relativization into account. In the literature,
her striving for the »natural‹ gesture of movement« is associated, among
other things, with the »entry into the natural space [...] or [...] cultural sites
of ancient Greek culture.« (Huschka 2002: 108) In addition to such descriptions, we are also familiar with early photographs of Duncan, one of which
shows her in the Parthenon Temple in Athens, for example, and was already
published in the first edition of *My Life* (1927: 348).[15] Our perception of this is
shaped in such a way that we can observe how she absorbs and transports
forces, as depicted in her gestures and her staging of space and light. These
images as sources cannot be examined in this chapter in greater detail, as
they are an entirely separate topic and study.[16] But suffice it to say that: particularly in the Greek episode of her autobiography, which is described as »a
pilgrim-age to the very holiest shrine of art« (Duncan 1927: 115f),[17] we witness
the spiritual Duncan as both a skeptic and even as an ironist. For example,
she does not fail to juxtapose the reported great amazement of the Greek
inhabitants, who wanted to »delight« in the strange behaviour of the dancing troops around Duncan, with a nonetheless pathetic depiction.[18] As au-

---

14 See also Duncan 1927, p. 77: »I also then dreamed of finding a first movement from which
    would be born a series of movements without my volition, but as the unconscious reac-
    tion of the primary movement.«
15 The image caption reads: »ISADORA DUNCAN. Standing in the west door of the Parthe-
    non (1920). From a photograph by Edward Steichen.«
16 For example, see Jahn/Wittrock/Wortelkamp 2015.
17 Duncan also writes in 1927, p. 115f: »We then revived a project which we had long cherished,
    of making a pilgrim-age to the very holiest shrine of art, of going to our beloved Athens.«
18 For example, see Duncan 2016, p. 111f. She also describes in Duncan 1927, p. 119f., 120 the
    »inhabitants who wanted to feast on us.« See also Ibid, p. 340: »it has often made me
    smile – but somewhat ironically – when people have called my dancing ›Greek‹, for I my-

thor she also exposes her own endeavors to reach the enduring experience of ›originality‹ as a »dazzling« yet now suddenly burst »soap bubble«:

Figure 1: ISADORA DUNCAN. Standing in the west door of the Parthenon (1920). From a photograph by Edward Steichen.

self count its origin in the stories which my Irish grandmother often told us of crossing the plains with grandfather in a covered wagon.«

> I ascended the Propylæa and stood before the Parthenon. Suddenly it seemed to me as if all our dreams burst like a glorious bubble, and we were not, nor ever could be, other than moderns. We could not have the feeling of the Ancient Greeks. This Temple of Athena before which I stood, had in other times known other colors. [...] The beautiful illusion of one year spent in Hellas seemed suddenly to break. (Duncan 1927: 134; Duncan 1928: 133)

She relativizes her entire quest for the original or the mythical in memory with the following reflective statement: »When I look back on this year spent in Greece I think it was really beautiful, this effort to reach back over two thousand years to a beauty not perhaps understood by us, or understandable by others.« (Duncan 1927: 134) The energetic, which Duncan mobilized in terms of Ancient Greece for her »so-called Greek Dance, with which [she has] flooded the world« (1927: 341), is something that she knows how to grasp just as well as the initiation and regulation of her own forces, as she describes retrospectively regarding, for example, music, or in the already quoted image of trembling palm leaves. I use this example to clarify that such juxtapositions and relativizations in autobiography do not contradict the simultaneous tendency toward the spiritual control of forces, which characterize research on Duncan's dance. However, what they do accomplish is the creation of a more complex representation of this historical figure in the history of dance, and therefore can impact our own conceptions of Duncan's understanding of dance and forces.

Energy Consumption (The Exhaustion of Forces)

Although Duncan was barely 50 years old when she wrote her autobiography and then passed away after an tragic accident, the life she describes is exceptionally rich in events, successes and failures, encounters, passions and tragic strokes of fate.[19] What is interesting in the context of this essay is that, for her, dance seems to be a source of strength autonomous from other circumstances.

---

19   See also Duncan 1927, p. 1, where she not incorrectly postulates: »Not that my life has not been more interesting than any novel and more adventurous than any cinema and, if really well written, would not be an epoch-making recital.«

For example, after the death of her children she writes: »Seeing what a tangled mesh of sorrow and catastrophe this life had brought me, in which only my idea always shone bright and untarnished above it all, I consented.« (Duncan 1927: 299) According to Duncan's self-portrayal, she does not consume those energies bundled in her inner being via her dance practice; rather these energies sometimes ebb, before becoming stronger once again. Passages in Graham and Bentley's works on energy consumption describe this relationship quite differently, which could be related to their own understandings of dance, as well as to differing mechanisms of discourse figurations of the energetic.

In 2003, 76 years after Duncan, Balanchine ballerina Toni Bentley crafts a completely different picture of her energy balance as a dancer. Using a very critical tone towards the ballet world, she describes an over-exploitation of forces, which is more or less voluntary, yet is also socially unparalleled and unrewarded. She writes:

> Yet college professors and government workers get pensions, and dancers do not. Our work is taken from us through no fault of our own, except maybe the fault of choosing to dance at all. But nobody warns a ten-year-old that he will be finished at forty, and what ten-year-old would listen? I doubt that even one of us would not choose to do it again, for we are believers. No dancer will deny the value, the total value, of his dedication. Who could ever say after giving so much of himself – more than ever conceived existed – that it was not the highest possible pursuit, to use and shape all one's energy to create beauty? (Bentley 2003: 51)

According to Bentley, consuming all of one's energy in order to create beauty is both the claim and the trap for ballet dancers, who inevitably pursue it because, after the exhaustion of their forces, nothing else remains for them.

If one compares the dance and the artistic environments of Duncan and Bentley, the difference becomes clear: while the latter as performer and thus ›giver‹ moves in the hierarchical ballet world, Duncan creates in and through herself. This also suggests a different discursive configuration of the energetic. Nevertheless, it is at least remarkable that Graham, whose creative aspects regarding the understanding of dance could certainly be placed closer

to Duncan's than Bentley's, argues alongside the latter Ballerina with regard
to her statements on energy consumption, for example when she writes:

> I wonder how long one can stay on fire. It is a curious fire. [...] At least I think
> I know what it does mean to burn slowly from within ... to feel so possessed
> by flame as to be infinitely hot and about to disintegrate into an ash at any
> instant. It may be very beautiful to watch. People here speak of my radiance,
> that I look as though I had found a new life ... Perhaps it is the final glow and
> not a beginning. (Graham 1991: 187)

Admittedly, the author was almost twice the age that Duncan ever reached
when she wrote this passage. It is therefore understandable that an almost
centenarian's own exhaustion of strength appears this painful, especially
when she writes: »I think I never want them [my students, C. T.] to be on
fire if it is so painful for them as it is for me.« (Graham 1991: 187) On the basis of this passage, however, I would like to make one last argument about
how statements on mobilized energies can help draw and make productive
dance-historiographical conclusions.

For Graham »this kind of energy« is a kind of stimulating spark, or »some animating spark« (1992: 50), which – according to her own description – must
be awakened, and which flickeringly burns for a dancer's entire life until finally – with the exhaustion of forces – it disappears again. In contrast, Duncan discursively depicts the relationship between dance and the energetic
quite differently, namely not as consumption, but as transposition. As described in the quote above, she attracts energies as »a kind of magnetic center« and internally processes them first as a »medium«, before transporting
them outwards again as an »emotional expression« (Duncan 1927: 224). Only
in this confrontation of two historical discourse figurations can different
conceptions of the energetic and its function be explored within a particular
understanding of dance – as this chapter has shown. How we can then approach the concrete dances of these two, or even of other dancers who have
articulated themselves similarly – each individually and at best only com-
paratively – would be, I argue, a worthwhile question to continue pursuing.

Works Cited

Bentley, Toni (2003): *Winter Season. A Dancer's Journal*, (Gainesville: University Press of Florida).

Boehm, Gottfried/Brandstetter, Gabriele/Müller, Achatz von (eds.) (2007): *Figur und Figuration. Studien zu Wahrnehmung und Wissen. Unter Mitarbeit von Maja Naef*, (Paderborn: Wilhelm Fink Verlag).

Brandl-Risi, Bettina/Ernst, Wolf-Dieter/Wagner, Meike (eds.) (2000): *Figuration. Beiträge zum Wandel der Betrachtung ästhetischer Gefüge*, (München: epodium).

Duncan, Isadora (2008): »Der Tanz der Zukunft.« In: Tzaneva, Magdalena (ed.): *Isadora Duncans Tanz der Zukunft. 130 Stimmen zum Werk von Isadora Duncan. Gedenkbuch zum 130. Geburtstg von Isadora Duncan, (27. May 1878 San Francisco – 14. September 1927 Nizza)*, (Berlin: LiDi). pp. 33-50.

Duncan, Isadora (1903): *Der Tanz der Zukunft. The dance of the future: Eine Vorlesung*, Karl Federn (trans.), (Leipzig: E. Diederichs).

Duncan, Isadora (2016): *I've only danced my life. Die Autobiografie der Isadora Duncan*, Ute Astrid Rall (trans.), (Berlin: Parthas Verlag).

Duncan, Isadora (1928): *Memoiren*, (Zürich, Leipzig and Wien: Amalthea Verlag).

Duncan, Isadora (1927): *My Life*, (New York: Boni & Liveright).

Duncan, Isadora (2013): *My Life, The restored edition with a new introduction by Joan Acocella*, (New York: Liveright).

Graham, Martha (1991): *Blood Memory*, (New York: Doubleday).

Graham, Martha (1992): *Der Tanz – mein Leben. Eine Autobiographie*, Dagmar Ahrens (trans.), (München: Wilhelm Heyne Verlag).

Holdenried, Michaela (2000): *Autobiographie*, (Stuttgart: Reclam).

Huschka, Sabine/Gronau, Barbara (2018): *Energetic Forces as Aesthetic Interventions. Wahrnehmungspolitiken von Körper/Szenen. Programm.* Symposium. https://www.tanz-wissen.de/images/dfg_symposium/Huschka-Symposium_Energetic-forces-as-aesthetic-interventions.pdf, May 24, 2018.

Huschka, Sabine (2000): *Merce Cunningham und der Moderne Tanz. Körperkonzepte, Choreographie und Tanzästhetik*, (Würzburg: Königshausen & Neumann).

Huschka, Sabine (2002): *Moderner Tanz. Konzepte - Stile - Utopien*, (Reinbek: rowohlts enzyklopädie).

Jahn, Tessa/Wittrock, Eike/Wortelkamp, Isa (eds.) (2015): *Tanzfotografie. Historiografische Reflexionen der Moderne: Tanzscripte 36*, (Bielefeld: Transcript).

Keller, Reiner (2011): *Wissenssoziologische Diskursanalyse. Grundlegung eines Forschungsprogramms*, (Wiesbaden: Springer).

Lejeune, Philippe (1994): *Der autobiographische Pakt*, (Frankfurt a.M.: Suhrkamp).

Plissezkaja, Maija (2006): *Ich, Maija: Die Primaballerina des Bolschoi-Theaters erzählt aus ihrem Leben*, Bernd Rullkötter (trans.), (Bergisch Gladbach: Bastei Lübbe).

Wagner-Egelhaaf, Martina (2005): *Autobiographie*, 2nd ed., (Stuttgart: J.B Metzler).

The ›Energetic‹ as Aesthetic:
Philosophical Approaches

Energetic Forces as Aesthetic Forces
The Doubling of Man and His Other

Gerald Siegmund

Sabine Huschka poses the following introductory questions for this volume: »What are we dealing with in terms of energetic forces? What exactly comes into view with the energetic as an aesthetic force?« (see Huschka/Gronau, Introduction to this volume). The answers I shall provide in this chapter are as follows: when we discuss energetic forces, we are dealing with a distinct understanding of the human being as a split being. When we consider energetic forces to be aesthetic forces, what is at stake is the capacity of energy »to mobilize, initiate, regulate and direct movement« (ibid.), which I argue is a double movement. Energy mobilizes and initiates movement to create and produce shapes and bodies, while it also dissolves and undoes both these shapes and figures as well as the social formations resulting from this shaping of movement. Energetic forces as aesthetic forces therefore simultaneously undo what they create, thus causing ambiguity and ambivalence in our emotional and intellectual responses to a dance piece.

In his 1966 book *The Order of Things* Michel Foucault reminds us that the birth of »man« comes along with the idea of a doubling or re-doubling of the figure of »man«. In his attempt to »investigate man in its entirety«, thinking runs the »risk of discovering what could never be reached by his reflection or even by his consciousness« (1966 [2005]: 355). »The unthought«, as Foucault describes this dark realm of man, with its »dim mechanisms, faceless determinations« is a »whole landscape of shadow« (ibid.). It remains »in relation to man, the Other: the Other that is not only a brother, but a twin, born, not of man, nor in man, but beside him and at the same time, in an identical newness, in an unavoidable duality« (ibid., 356). This double or split produces the figure of the twin or a *Doppelgänger* haunting 19th century literature, from E.T.A. Hoffmann's story *The Sandman* to Robert Lewis Stevenson's almost paradigmatic narrative of *Dr. Jekyll and Mr. Hyde*. The double, as Foucault argues, in fact constitutes the ground for the possibility that »man« has an interior space, and that this interior, like Nietzsche's notion of the Dionysian or Freud's discovery of the unconscious, anthropologically speaking, is a »dark force« from which the imagination or the phantasy (*Einbildungskraft*) springs. This imagination is productive and creative in undoing and redoing images. On the other hand, if taken seriously, this redoubled space is also the residue of a force that undoes the man of reason by threatening his integrity. Confronting him with what he does not know or cannot experience, this energetic force pushes him into the unknown territory of himself. For Foucault, the realm of man's experience therefore co-emerges with the field of the unknown:

> The question is no longer: How can experience of nature give rise to necessary judgements? But rather: How can man think what he does not think, inhabit as though by a mute occupation something that eludes him, animate with a kind of frozen movement that figure of himself that takes the form of a stubborn exteriority? How can men *be* that life whose web, pulsations, and buried energy constantly exceed the experience that he is immediately given of them? (Foucault 2005: 352)

Foucault uses metaphors of movement, energy, and pulsation to describe the other side of man, which, as a field of knowledge, he labels »existence«. This is opposed to the Kantian »science of nature« that finds its certainties in laws of nature. For Foucault, existence as the field of transcendental reflection in its modern form is »mute, yet ready to speak, and secretly impregnated with a potential discourse – of that *not-known* from which man is permanently summoned towards self-knowledge« (ibid: 352). Energy thus exceeds the immediately given, and opens man up to an exteriority that he may also find within himself. Foucault situates the rise of phenomenology as a philosophical discipline in the doubling of man. »The phenomenological project continually resolves itself, before our eyes, into a description – empirical despite itself – of actual experience, and into an ontology of the unthought that automatically short-circuits the primacy of the ›I think‹« (ibid: 355).

If dance can be described as the expenditure and shaping of energy, phenomenology's »ontology of the unthought« is, I posit, ideally located within the field of dance and its work on and with the body as a site that eludes the sole rationale of the cogito. It allows us to rediscover, make visible, and experience what is inherent to existence: the forces, pulsations, and energies that make us exist. That is to say: to stand apart from ourselves, outside of our cognitive selves. It leads us into a realm where thinking is momentarily suspended because we encounter that which we have not yet thought or known. Since the early 19th century, dance reformulates its premises as a form bringing that »mute, yet ready to speak« side of man to the fore. It allows for transgressions into the unthought, thus preparing the ground for transformations, while also providing a conscious and known shape to the unknown.

Therefore, access to this »exteriority« – an invention that is tied to the invention of »man« or the »human« since the latter part of the 18th century – becomes a move of transgression towards that which cannot be known or thought, and which, strictly speaking, cannot be fully experienced. Transgression as an act potentially leads to a transformation into that exteriority, which is the other side of »man« while being inevitably connected to him. In this elusive field, all kinds of transformations of »man« into his other are possible. Transformations between animals and humans (*Swan Lake*), between the living and the dead (*Giselle*), between man and woman, between the organic and the machine-like (*Coppélia*) haunt the very being of romantic or classical ballet (cf. also Brandstetter 2017). As I have argued elsewhere (Siegmund 2010), *Giselle* achieved this transformation via a revolution of perception that engulfed the spectator in a dream-like vision of white muslin, which would inevitably dissolve the clear physical shapes of the dancers' bodies into pure visuality. Today, danced transgressive acts seek to directly access the (somatic) interior exteriority of man, thus minimizing the representation of bodies and making them fluid (arguably without taking shape). Unlike in *Giselle*, these produce a physical rather than a visual effect. They articulate affective bodies, and aim to impact the audience on a visceral and emotional level short-circuiting reason. Nonetheless, in both instances the logic behind the search for the hidden potentials of the dancing body remains the same. The ›truth‹ (of »man«, the body, or movement) is still ›out there‹ in the exterior interior of the human being.

Discussing energetic forces today still relies on the same idea of man's double, the emergence of which, as a distinct type of knowledge, makes us think what we cannot think (Foucault 2005: 352). Despite their different kinesthetic premises and their specific ways of regulating the transition from exterior to interior spaces, following Foucault current somatic practices are not distinct from the practices of shaping untapped interior forces as sources of energy for movement. However, what becomes apparent when discussing energetic forces as aesthetic forces, which is what I will do now, is a special quality that does not merely mobilize, activate, regulate or direct movement. At the same time that energy gives rise to movement, bodies, and actions, it separates that which it creates from itself. It is here that the aesthetic dimension of energetic forces resides. In the following I will present this double activity of doing and undoing as that which becomes apparent when we consider energetic forces to be aesthetic forces. In his writings, the late American dance scholar and sociologist Randy Martin understands dance as a mobilizing force that is also effective in the social and political realm. I confront his reading of dance as a mobilizing force with its aesthetic side: the undoing of form, for which I will refer to the ideas of the German philosopher Christoph Menke. I agree with Menke that mobilization as a force is constitutive for the subject as an aesthetic subject. Being an aesthetic subject entails being transgressive, because the subject that comes into being by discipline, due to its twin double, always exceeds the very practices that brought it into being (Menke 2003). I conclude by briefly mapping out some of dance's potential for transgression and transformation today.

Mobilization

In his seminal book *Critical Moves. Dance Studies in Theory and Politics* (1998) Martin proposes rethinking the relation between dance and politics, based on his concept of mobilization. He inquires as to what dance and its study can offer to politics, given that both are already forms of articulating the social. For Martin, the dynamics of mobilization are already inherent in politics, although political theory includes very little reflection on its implications (1998: 4). On the other hand, the dynamics of mobilization are just as crucial in bringing about a dance performance: gathering together performers and members of the audience alike. For Martin, dance therefore resonates with what he calls »the entire social kinesthetic« (ibid: 24). Mobilization traverses diverse social, artistic and political practices, shaping and connecting bodies creating agency and difference along the way. Therefore, as the French philosopher Jacques Rancière pointed out twelve years later, art and politics do not reside in separate spheres. One rather needs to conceptualize their primary connection as being embedded or enfolded in the raw material of our sensory world. Art and politics shape and distribute sensory experience as both legible and sensate in their own rights, and as ways to their own ends and needs, with the former re-distributing and re-negotiating what the latter has posited as hegemonic (Rancière 2010: 148-149).

Martin conceptualizes the relationship between dance and politics as one of mobilization rather than resistance. Mobilization is a force that helps to articulate the relationship between dance and politics in a positive and productive way (Martin 1998: 13). To Martin, politics are already shaping the world, and, like dance, they are a collision and displacement of forces that produce difference. As opposed to existing readings of the word »mobilization«, Martin conceives of it as not being subject to efficacy or the particular interest of specific social groups. Mobilization is rather something that precedes its own usage. »If movement can be plotted on a grid of space and time, mobilization is what generates the grid«, Martin explains (ibid: 4). Mobilization is instrumental in creating and preserving »a space where new formations germinate« (ibid: 13). »Hence«, Martin continues, »through mobilization, bodies traverse a given terrain that by traversing, they constitute« (ibid: 4). Mobilization draws upon forces and contexts from beyond the realm of the given performance (political, economic, conceptual, and aesthetic), and assembles them in one space, so as to work with and upon them. Already in this sense, it separates movements, bodies and their actions from themselves. Like a dance production, it unites dancers ready to participate in the creation of a choreography with members of the audience ready to attend the performance. Mobilization is thus situated »between production and product« (ibid): a dynamic that underlies the various analyses that Martin conducts in the individual chapters of his book. The production side assembles a »capacity for movement«, whereas the side of the product highlights the materialization of identities »accomplished through the performance« (ibid). Mobilization produces agency, which is ultimately conducive to the imagination of any political project by concentrating on the process of »how bodies are made« (ibid). Since mobilization is not movement *per se*, but rather the »capacity for movement«, it must, however, operate on a different level than movement. It thus becomes a vector of energy, and stimulates bodies and their movements to take a certain direction. As such, it is the potential for action that, by principle, may choose any direction. This is ongoing and hard to contain, and so directing and limiting it becomes the task of the dynamic between the production and the product of the dance.

Force

On re-reading the passages on mobilization in *Critical Moves*, one is struck by the realization that Martin was quite aware of what else was at stake, and that mobilization as a concept threatened to offer more than he sought to find. »By mobilization I want to stress not an alien power that is visited on the body, as something that is done to bodies behind their backs, so to speak, but what moving bodies can accomplish through movement.« (ibid: 4) As a sociologist and political theorist, Martin was certainly not interested in what went on behind peoples' backs, especially because he focused instead on social change and on the making of bodies to instigate that change. If mobilization is neither identical with the movement it facilitates nor the bodies it creates and deploys spatially, then one must inquire where else it might originate from, if not behind the body's back. When applying Foucault's idea of »man«, it might be inquired if this power is not alien to the body itself, which neither mind nor body can fully grasp apart from the effects it produces on those bodies. Although Martin shied away from comparing his concept to what Freud called the residue of the drive, or what Nietzsche metaphorically described as the Dionysian side of the production of art, mobilization nonetheless resonates with both of these concepts. It therefore places the bodies and the new forms of subjectivity that it itself produces at risk once again.

In this moment of uncertainty, Menke's conception of »force« as a dark power, or to use Foucault's image, »a whole landscape of shadow« (2005: 355) gains significance. As a philosopher of aesthetics, Menke is not primarily interested in social change, but rather in the notion of equality associated with art since the Enlightenment. His claims about force also assert the basic freedom of human beings. This is why art is political: neither freedom nor equality are given. »Man is neither free nor equal by nature« Menke argues, referring to Hannah Arendt's »prepolitical state of nature, which is«, as Menke points out, »nevertheless a social state: the economic, technical, cultural state of ›society‹, the life of ›private citizens‹.« (Menke 2011: 11) In this social state we acquire capacities by learning, and we gain skills by training, which transforms us into human beings able to successfully participate in society.

However, this process of acquisition also implies that some skills are worth more than others. Those applying them are graded according to normative values and binaries: worthy/worthless, useful/useless, abled/disabled etc. »Our capacities socialize but also disunite us. They are fields for and objects of struggle.« (ibid: 12) However noble this struggle of capacities may be in some respects, it nonetheless cannot become the site of equality, because these capacities are never neutral in their value. Menke rejects the more popular view that the struggle for political equality resides in the emancipation of all productive differences from other, less favorable, distinctions. He instead argues that true emancipation lies in the freedom from »the differences that constitute our abilities«, i.e. from our socially acquired capacities and abilities (ibid: 13). Provocatively, I have called this a move from difference to »in-difference« in my essay for *The Oxford Handbook* (Siegmund 2017). Instead of grounding the idea of equality in the emancipation of differences, it is rather located at a more fundamental level where differences do not yet exist, where there is an indifference to difference, and where human beings are equal in force. Aesthetics is the ideal realm where subjects may experience the force of their own undoing.

Menke therefore seeks that which facilitates capacities, which essentially is force. Force is ontologically different from capacities, as otherwise it would fall prey to the production of individual differences.

> *Capacities* make us subjects who successfully partake in social practices. In the play of *force*, we are presubjective and metasubjective agents but not subjects; active without self-consciousness, inventive without goal. [...] Equality, as equality of force, is nothing given. Force, in which we are equal, is a presupposition, because it is there for us, we experience and know of it only by performing acts in which it unfolds. Such acts are aesthetic; acts of play, of imagination. (Menke 2011: 14-15)

The *potential* of our political equality is primarily an aesthetic freedom, aesthetics being the field of potentiality in which forces manifest themselves *without ends as forces*.

Force and mobilization align by being the grid rather than the movement, and being the potential to move rather than movement in space and time. They are rallying calls for change and transformation, and for different articulations of bodies and social kinesthetic energies. They are both *impersonal* non-subjectified vehicles for an open process of doing and undoing. The im-personal, pre-subjective tears the personal and subjective apart. Dance for Martin »concentrates on the social forces that make bodies what they are« (Martin 1998: 24). Following Menke, dance makes us experience the forces that make bodies *not* what they are, although during the performance they clearly *are* something. Art makes us unlearn what we have learned socially, and makes us do what we cannot do, which leads to the production of an unforeseen event. What Menke points out is that force never allows the body to settle, even in the form it has assumed. What Martin fails to realize by avoiding looking at what happens »behind [the body's] back« is the undoing of what capacities have created. To radicalize Martin's notion of mobiliza-tion, one can say that mobilization *never stops*, even when dancers and audi-ences have gathered and joined forces. The move between production and the product that mobilization triggers never results only in the physical materi-alization of identities and the production of differences. It also always and *at the very same time and by the very same gesture* results in a move of dis-identifi-cation, or, as Judith Butler argues with Foucault, of »de-subjugation« (2004). In order to become political, political mobilizations have to cease mobilizing for a certain cause. They produce surplus effects that cannot be subjected to a certain cause. These effects undo what mobilization has created (bodies, actions), using the very force that drives it on. Mobilization allows us to sur-pass the limits of our knowledge, or as Foucault articulates it, of the primacy of the »I think« (Foucault 2005: 355). These transgressions into the unknown allow for a re-shaping or a transformation of both experience and knowledge. Appealing to the duality of both terms, transgression represents the dissolv-ing of experience, while transformation emphasizes its re-formulation.

Transformation

However, these ideas must also be criticized. In a massive act of de-subju-gation, a significant portion of contemporary Continental dance over the last 15-20 years was characterized by the unlearning of techniques, the un-doing of representations of the body, and the reception of social interaction as epitomized in the audience-dancer relationship. Contemporary dance was thereby often also labeled as »conceptual dance«, as it was engaged in acts of criticism that produced unforeseen instances of the possibilities of dance. However, producing the unforeseen by abandoning what one confidently knows is precisely what creative capitalism desires, according to the social and political philosophy dedicated to analyzing the »new spirit of capitalism« (Boltanski and Chiapello: 2017). To keep capital afloat we must ourselves ›flow‹, thereby assuming ever mobile and precarious existences. New forms of subjectivity are immediately commoditized in order to create new markets. As Bojana Kunst points out in her book *Artist at Work*, »subjectivity is at the core of human production [...] and capital powers deeply affect the powers and potentialities of life« (Kunst 2015: 41). Creative capitalism consumes subjectivities and their forces, in order to transgress and transform them. What was held to be an act of emancipation, during the heyday of performance art in the 1960s and 1970s, today only serves »contemporary post-Fordist production [...] One's work is intertwined with the performance and maintenance of creativity« (ibid: 42), which is the primary source of revenue for neo-liberal capitalism. So what are we to do? I argue that the powers of mobilization, as Martin theorized them, produce something worth our time and attention, regardless of how precarious and ambivalent the results may be. Movement materializes and carves out places for the subject to speak, move, or act. I maintain that the notion of subjectivity is not the same in dance as in capitalist production. According to Giorgio Agamben, the work of creative capitalism, including all of its technical tools and gadgets, is to destroy subjectivity (Agamben 2009: 20). Subjectivities cannot assume a form anymore because contemporary technology short-circuits the wish for the Other, along with the promise of its instant gratification via consumer goods, and, perhaps even more so, via images. It therefore erases both memory and imagination as necessary capacities for forming subjects. In doing so, it replaces subjects with consumer zombies. It destroys desire. On the other hand, by means of desire »man« holds onto older formations as a way of knowing the subject, which goes beyond instant gratification.

Desire is thus distinct from the wish, and whereas neo-liberal consumer capitalism thrives on the wish, dance works with desire. Although neo-liberal consumer capitalism promises to fulfill one's every wish, inevitably a new item to be consumed soon appears. In contrast, desire remains faithful to its object precisely because it cannot own it. Something clings to desire, which crosses out its contemporaneity. Instead, it is already so *passé* once it emerges that it promises to drag the past into the future. This is precisely because it creates an indefinite object that, even after countless failures, it will always resurrect and remain faithful to. It is worth noting that Martin conceives of the body primarily as »the seat of desire«. He sees desire as »the physical agent of activity« (Martin 1985: 56), which is forever responding to and effecting change on the environment, as Susan Leigh Foster puts it in one of her essays (2016). The body as a desiring body, which is ready to affect and be affected, may be mobilized to move. And, it is critical to note, it thus requires a moment of dis-identification. It also demands an instance of impersonality and pre-subjectivity, as well as a period of what I have called in-difference to difference, before it can begin moving at all. It needs to undo first, before it can start redoing. Once mobilization has set bodies in motion, its surplus force prevents an identitarian closure of the scene created by movement. Only when the product of mobilization and its work prevents those subjects formed and endowed with agency from ever becoming a self-identical subject can mobilization as a moment of force *continue to effect change*. This is what art accomplishes. Mobilization thus conceptualized indicates a moment of rupture, which produces an opening propelling social subjectivity forward, precisely because, for the period of the performance, they have become aesthetic subjects *equal* in both force and in their power to transform. Aesthetic subjects are divided because they do not know what goes on behind their backs, yet they can be carried away by the results of mobilization. They are never entirely in control of what they do, show, or try to achieve. That is why their performance is both risky and open to new social formations, even beyond the stage.

In order to articulate subjectivity differently, mobilization requires a moment of de-subjectivation or dis-identification before it can resist hegemonic forms of governance. The form of subjectivity produced by mobilization therefore contrasts the form of subjectivity *not* destroyed by consumer capitalism. Instead it becomes momentarily suspended or expanded, and hovers in mid-air to be analyzed and re-formed. I have argued that the political dimension of the aesthetic resides in the ambivalences and ambiguities created by a dance piece. The product plays with its own limits and operating contexts. It calls our judgment into question by opening up multiple points of view, but without ever settling on one. Therefore, the work of art may not be consumed because it is always over- and under-determined. One wishes to return to attend the performance again and again. Even after countless failings, the desire for dance remains strong. The bodies mobilized for movement will always sink back into themselves as opaque and resistant, while at the same time they remain instilled with the imagination and potentials for movement. They are resurrected in each performance, and while they are here, they are also never quite ›here‹, but rather ›over there‹ on some kind of stage, wherever it may be. This intertwines presence with an inexhaustible absence that may not be consumed but can only be desired. Therefore, the object of art or dance appeals to both memory and imagination as two human capacities allowing an ongoing engagement with the performance. This is also the sense in which performance *remains* (Schneider 2011). Desire is faith in the object, or, in this case, the dance, and it implies an ethical dimension.

Works Cited

Agamben, Giorgio (2009): »What is an Apparatus?« In: *What is an Apparatus? and Other Essays*, David Kishik and Stefan Pedatella (trans.), (Stanford: Stanford University Press), pp. 1-24.

Boltanski, Luc/Chiapello, Ève (2017 [1999]): *The New Spirit of Capitalism*, Gregory Elliott (trans.), (London and New York: Verso).

Brandstetter, Gabriele (2017): »Human, Animal, Thing. Shifting Boundaries in Modern and Contemporary Dance«. In: Gabriele Brandstetter/Holger Hartung (eds.): *Moving (Across) Borders. Performing Translation, Intervention, Participation*, (Bielefeld: transcript), pp. 23-42.

Butler, Judith. (2004): »What is Critique? An Essay on Foucault's Virtue. In: Sara Salih/Judith Butler (eds.): *The Judith Butler Reader*, (Oxford: Blackwell), pp. 302-322.

Foster, Susan Leigh (2016): »Why Is There Always Energy for Dance?«, *Dance Research* Journal 48/3, pp. 12-26.

Foucault, Michel (2005 [1966]): *The Order of Things*, (London and New York: Routledge).

Kunst, Bojana (2015): *Artist at Work. Proximity of Art and Capitalism*, (Winchester and Washington: Zero Books).

Martin, Randy (1985): »Dance as Social Movement«, *Social Text* 12/3, pp. 54-70.

Martin, Randy (1998): *Critical Moves. Dance Studies in Theory and Politics*, (Durham and London: Duke University Press).

Menke, Christoph (2003): »Die Disziplin der Ästhetik. Eine Lektüre von ›Überwachen und Strafen‹«. In: Gertrud Koch (ed.): *Kunst als Strafe. Zur Ästhetik der Disziplinierung*, (München: Wilhelm Fink), pp. 109-121.

Menke, Christoph (2011): *Aesthetics of Equality/Ästhetik der Gleichheit*, Christopher Jenkin-Jones (trans.), (Ostfildern, Germany: Hatje Cantz Verlag).

Rancière, Jacques (2010): »The Paradox of Political Art«. In: Steven Corcoran (ed.): *Dissensus. On Politics and Aesthetics*, Steven Corcoran (trans.), (London and New York: Continuum Books), pp. 134-151.

Schneider, Rebecca. (2011): *Performing Remains. Art and War in Times of Theatrical Reenactment*, (London and New York: Routledge).

Siegmund, Gerald (2010): »Giselle, oder: das Sehen auf dem Weg in die Moderne«. In: Claudia Jeschke/Nicole Haitzinger (eds.): *Tanz & Archiv: ForschungsReisen*, Band 3, Historiographie, (München: epodium Verlag), pp. 120-129.

Siegmund, Gerald (2017): »Rehearsing In-Difference: The Politics of Aesthetics in the Performances of Pina Bausch and Jérôme Bel«. In: Rebekah Kowal/Randy Martin/Gerald Siegmund (eds.): *The Oxford Handbook of Dance and Politics*, (New York: Oxford University Press), pp. 181-198.

An earlier version of this paper was published in *Dance Research Journal* 48/3 (December 2016).

Cosmology of Forces, Performative Fields

Maximilian Haas

The networked ensembles of bodies, media and objects – in short: the infrastructure – of a theatrical situation engenders and maintains a peculiar ecology of events, processes, and practices, not all of which are conducted by humans. This general characterization of theater as an art form of time-based assemblages is emphasized and placed at center-stage in a variety of recent dance and performance productions. These programmatically engage with non-human actors, such as machines and algorithms, animals, plants, and mere things, and sometimes even leave the entire stage to them.[1] Yet, what defines and distinguishes these modes of being? What lets us speak about them as such? What do humans, animals, plants, mere things, and machines have in common? What differentiates them? How do they appear and relate to each other? These questions are in fact issues of cosmology. ›Cosmology‹ refers to the philosophical discipline that addresses being as a whole. It conceives of the world as a natural order of physical substances and biological processes, and practically coincides with natural philosophy since the Greeks. Despite their apparent opposition along the nature-culture divide, cosmology and theater intersect and correspond to the extent that a) theater comprises of diverse bodies and processes that fall into the categories mentioned above (which is, of course, always the case), and b) cosmological thinking is facilitated through aspects and metaphors of theater (which is surprisingly often the case).

---

1 In the following I will use ›theater‹ generically as a signifier for the situational, architectur-
al, institutional, i.e. the striated spatio-temporal (pre-)conditions under which we experience performing arts in general. This naturally includes all forms of post-dramatic theater,
performance, and dance, the latter of which form a special focus here. Similarly, by »performance« I refer to all theatrical presentations regardless of their specification as (post-)
dramatic, dance, or performance art.

Yet, especially when it comes to performances that highlight the role of non- or more-than-human actors, and in which thus the differences and similarities between diverse modes of being are brought to the fore, one needs to theoretically account for the cosmological conditions and relations that usually remain implicit as fundamental premises of approach towards theatrical performances. Making these conditions and relations explicit in cosmological discussion can help to alter classical modern understandings of theater, which focus exclusively on human problems and intentions as the sole and only origin and cause, aim and purpose of performative events, processes, and practices. Accordingly, this essay brings together speculative approaches in natural philosophy that point towards another, less anthropocentric, view of the reality of theater. They propose a way of thinking about non/human actors in a performance situation that does not originate from their definition as either human, animal, plant, thing, or machine, but rather from the particular forces they are endowed with. For, it is the very notion of force that allows one to conceive of these diverse modes of being on equal ontological footing, while also accounting for the different ways and intensities with which force is organized and expressed in each case.

The concept of force is historically well-known to both natural philosophy and aesthetic theory, whose general definitions will be discussed here first in order to weigh their potentials and limitations for an aesthetic cosmology of forces. This aesthetic cosmology will be outlined then by drawing on the concepts and examples of two modern cosmological thinkers: mathematician and pragmatist philosopher Alfred North Whitehead, and philosopher of science and technology Gilbert Simondon. Their writings appeal to performance aesthetics, because they allow the relation between an individual and its milieu to be construed both as co-constitutive and emergent, as well as rooted in specific constellations of forces producing particular effects. They are thus based on two fundamental principles that also condition theatrical performance: relationality and processuality. In theatrical performances, an individual cannot be understood as such, but only in relation to the surrounding milieu and course of action. As these relations are intrinsically dynamic, one needs to systematically take into account their potential for change and transformation, which is precisely what the concept of force allows for. Furthermore, and more fundamentally, one needs to account for the fact that the individual would not be this individual without and beyond this very milieu and course of action, i.e. for the ontological (or, more precisely, the ontogenetic) dimension of dynamic relations. These views, however, rest at the heart of Whitehead's and Simondon's speculative approaches to and propositions in natural philosophy. Furthermore, they are developed here in regard to aesthetic understandings of concepts such as information and expression. Yet, modern cosmology does not only provide the concepts and examples of this essay but also its method, which shall be outlined incipiently.

Cosmology of Performance

Methodologically, a cosmological discussion of performance can be based upon Whitehead's peculiar *Essay in Cosmology* developed in his Gifford lectures on *Process and Reality* (published in 1929), wherein he construes the cosmological method as a mode of speculative philosophy. This touches upon metaphysics to the extent that it necessarily transcends the epistemic capacities and subject areas of the sciences and the humanities alike. Cosmology thus experimentally undoes what Whitehead calls the »bifurcation of nature«, i.e. the division of the world into two separate realms of being, which are conceived of according to fundamentally different criteria, and which ultimately lead to the ontological dualism of nature and culture, as well as the mutually exclusive epistemologies of the natural sciences and the humanities. However, this undoing cannot be safely grounded on fundamental principles because the principles at hand are generally fundamental only to one side of the ontological divide: nature or culture. Cosmological thinking therefore necessarily transgresses existing modes and areas of methodological thinking in academic disciplines.

However unsafe, there is a proper method for cosmology, which Whitehead characterizes as the »extensive abstraction« of concepts. By progressive detachment from the concrete, concepts developed in a particular science are made transferable to other areas of research and applicable to the realities they bring to the fore. Since the abstraction of the concept from the original object and its concretization in respect to another both exceed the methods of the respective sciences, the conceptual extension requires speculative intuition and imagination. These faculties, however, belong less to the sciences as such, but rather to philosophy as a conceptual mediator between them. The procedure is conceived of as experimental: whether a concept will be effective in this or that context cannot be determined until it has been tested there. As cosmological thinking thus necessarily leaves the foundation of proven knowledge to be represented by the specialist sciences, it becomes an »adventure« (Whitehead 1968: 173).

Although the aesthetic plays an important role in his cosmology, Whitehead does not consider artistic practices to be a cosmological means here.[2] Despite his own attempts in *Science and the Modern World* (Whitehead 1948) to base a philosophy of science partly on romantic poetry (ibid: 75-95), in *Process and Reality* the speculative construction of a relation between disparate realities is conceived of as a rational coordination of concepts. Yet one can argue that artistic practice is the very model of the speculative philosophizing that Whitehead proposes here as a cosmological method.[3] Following this argument, one could complement his cosmology with an aesthetic approach that integrates artistic practices and works of art as empirical test sites for notions of natural philosophy, which might, in turn, shed new light on these practices and works. Of course, it is *not* the aim of such a project to *explain* the nature of theater by means of concepts and theories derived from the natural sciences, i.e. to reduce its complex forms and functions to handy ex-

---

2 For Whitehead, the aesthetic comes into play as the systematic counterpart to logic. Logic and aesthetics form the two poles of abstraction, conceived of as a meaning-making relation between the empirical and the rational. They mediate between the part and the whole in opposite ways: logic proceeds from details and constructs a uniform scheme to contain them. On the contrary, the object of aesthetics – the work of art – initially presents itself as a unit that unfolds its complexity through time. Both logic and aesthetics utilize the vital tension between the part and the whole, albeit from opposite sides. »If either side of this antithesis sinks into the background, there is trivialization of experience, logical and aesthetic.« (Whitehead 1968: 60) Logic and aesthetics thus presuppose each other and practically depend on one another.

3 Although Whitehead's cosmology bases itself on rational logic, the author's sympathy lies with aesthetics. Here the relationship between part and whole is less constrained: In contrast to logic, in which the parts are completely absorbed in their function for the whole (3+3=6), in aesthetics they retain a stubborn disparity. »The whole displays its component parts, each with its own value enhanced; and the parts lead up to a whole, which is beyond themselves, and yet not destructive of themselves.« (Whitehead 1968: 62) Hence, it is not a negative judgment when Whitehead remarks: »Even the greatest works of art fall short of perfection.« (Ibid) This shortfall guarantees the liveliness of art, as well as its creativity in bridging disparate realities, which is, according to Whitehead, the very function of cosmological thinking. Furthermore, unlike logic, art can also express the process of realization that for Whitehead constitutes the very essence of reality.

planations that bear the authority of proven facts. On the contrary, cultural practices and natural processes should be placed into a relation of mutual critique, in order to unsettle conventional approaches to them and to foster a broader and richer understanding of both.

However, despite, or rather, because of its (ultimately) general character, cosmological thinking must be specified under certain aspects or concepts. In this essay it shall be located under the notion of force.

Force in Recent Aesthetic Theory

Force is a key concept in the philosophy of nature. But it is also important for the aesthetic theory of performance and performativity. The concept is used here to mark the difference between the *mise-en-scène* (*Inszenierung*) and the performance (*Aufführung*), or respectively between the choreography and the dance, i.e. between the structural and the performative dimensions of a theatrical piece. The actual performance will always be different, if not even ›more‹, than the decisions taken by the artists in the production. It cannot be reduced to artistic intentions afterwards, nor deduced from them before-hand, precisely because the actual, presented whole is more than the sum of its prefabricated parts, to use a vitalistic truism. However, the cause, name and measure of this illusive ›more‹ is force.

Erika Fischer-Lichte, for example, allocates force (or »power« respectively) to the theatrical dimension of presence and in opposition to theatrical representation, which is decisive for her conception of performativity (2008). The performative force of presence is the source and locus of theatrical performance as a *live* art form. According to Fischer-Lichte, theater owes this power to ritual, and it is this heritage that endows it with its two main faculties: the subversive and transformative (ibid: 154). Performative force acts subversively on the apparatus of theatrical production and presentation, including the *mise-en-scène* or choreography, but also on social codes and norms. The transformative force rather concerns the individuals or subjects involved (both performers and audience members) as well as the theatrical situation as a whole. Ideally, the transformation of oneself always also entails the transformation of others (and vice versa), thus contributing to the co-transformation of all the performance's parts, which is to say: the performance as a whole. Hence, performative force is conceived of as contagious. But in classic theories and aesthetics of performativity, it can always be traced back to the individual who produced it. »The ›magic‹ of presence«, Fischer-Lichte states:

> lies in the performer's particular ability to generate energy so that it can be sensed by the spectators as it circulates in space and affects, even tinges, them. This energy constitutes the force emanating from the performer. Insofar as it animates the spectators to generate energy themselves, they will perceive the actor as a source of power. This unexpected energy flow thus transforms actor and spectator alike. (Fischer-Lichte 2008: 96)

However, as we will see in the following cosmological discussion, force might not be adequately conceived of as an individual product. It rather calls for the logic of a dynamically organized field that enables its elements to perform.

Force was recently reassessed as a »fundamental concept« of »aesthetic anthropology«: Christoph Menke's two books offer an interesting reading of the notion of force in modern philosophy and aesthetics (2013a, 2013b). He positions the concept against the reduction of the experience of art to the faculties of a subject. Unlike subjective faculties, forces are obscure, alien factors that (de-)constitute the human in an impersonal play of expressions (2013a: 31-48). In developing this position historically, Menke also draws upon natural philosophy, although only as applied to human nature. This is a logical consequence of Menke's attempt at an »aesthetic anthropology«, i.e. a theory of human aesthetics and, more importantly, an aesthetic theory of the human. An aesthetic cosmology of forces could partially draw on the same historical positions that Menke does. And it would also position itself towards the relation between human and nature, which offers a criticism of modern philosophy's rationalist obsession with the subject. Yet, it would not single out Man from nature, but rather would conceive of human experience and practice as being of and in nature – including those related to art and aesthetics. This is because, from a cosmological perspective, art and aesthetics cannot be seen to be an exception or a practical negation of nature, but rather as a peculiar self-reflexive form of it, as they are comprised of natural substances and bodies, as well as of their respective potentials and activities. Working on the relation between the human and nature from different angles, anthropological approaches to aesthetics, such as Menke's, as well as cosmological ones can be conceived of as complementary projects to one another.

In comparison with classic performative aesthetics, a cosmology of performative forces can open up a less anthropocentric perspective on theater. This perspective would not be centered around the individual, but rather oriented towards the situational ontogenesis of performative events, the becoming of form through distributed force, i.e. a field-logics of performance. In order to validate the plausibility of this reorientation, we must first trace the conception of force in the history of natural philosophy. This will allow conceptual oppositions – mechanistic/teleological, analytical/synthetical, objective/subjective, individual/environmental – to eventually be contained in a cosmological understanding of force.

Force in Natural Philosophy

Force is the ability to move, to transform, and to make a change. Generally speaking it forms the bond between cause and effect. Throughout its history, force underwent different conceptual constellations in respect to the closely related notions of energy and power. The concept has an anthropomorphic origin: the Aristotelian *dynamis* is derived from the human senses of effort and will that accompany a purposeful and intentional action. This teleological understanding of force, extended to nonhuman forces and prevalent until the Middle Ages, was juxtaposed with a mechanistic understanding in the early days of modern physics. Although Johannes Kepler initially regards the physical forces guiding the celestial bodies along their orbits as *anima*, i.e. as souls who animate the planets, he soon developed techniques for their calculation. Isaac Newton thereafter applies the physically path-breaking formula »mass x acceleration.« In doing so, he reduces force to the objectively determinable and measurable quantities of an inert substance, which occupies a discrete place in space, as well as to an aimless and purposeless movement, which is divisible by arbitrary periods of time.

This quantitative analysis of force, which is tantamount to its logical dissociation into isolable elements, raises philosophical issues. With his concept of striving forces, which behave like Aristotelian entelechies,[4] Gottfried Wilhelm Leibniz proposes an understanding of force as a synthesis across space and time. According to this conception, a force cannot be assigned a discrete point in space and time, as it always goes beyond itself. Spatially, it extends to the things and situations it influences. Temporally, it stretches into the future of its effects. Therefore, a force essentially reaches beyond itself, bringing itself into unity with the ›other‹ on which it operates. Forces are synthetical by nature – a nature that their discrete analysis necessarily fails to acknowledge (Leibniz 1998, 1991).

The mechanistic and the teleological understandings of force are opposed to each other in many ways, yet both are based on two fundamental assumptions: the individual and elusive character of force. The latter relates to the fact that a force does not appear as such, but rather manifests itself only in its effects. What we call a force is actually an abstractive objectification of change, the logical detachment of transformation away from the concrete and conceptual absolutization and into an individual entity. It is for this very reason that the history of the concept is accompanied by the question of whether or not force actually exists. Is force an objective factor to be found empirically in real entities and situations? Or is that which we call ›force‹ nothing more than a crutch for logical thinking; a rational fiction that only prevailed in the history of science because it allowed for the formal understanding of physical problems?[5]

---

4 Aristotle introduces the concept of entelechy in his *Metaphysics* (IX, 8). It describes the form which is realized in the matter, especially in the sense of an inherent power of the organism which brings it to self-realization.

5 The neo-Kantian philosopher Hans Vaihinger writes (following Taine): »If two events, one preceding, the other following, are united by a constant bond, we call that peculiarity of the antecedent event, which consists in its being followed by another event, its ›force,‹ and we measure this force in terms of magnitude of its effect. In reality only sequences and coexistences exist and we ascribe ›forces‹ to things, by regarding the actual phenomena as already possible and then hypostasizing these possibilities and peculiarities, and separating them from the rest as real entities.« (Vaihinger 1935: 197) However, the author does not dismiss the concept of force at all, but rather emphasizes the fruitful role it nonetheless played in the history of physics. Interestingly, he furthermore stresses the psychological dimension of the concept: To the extent that forces »are raised to the rank of substances and placed as the permanent background, as a constant fountain-head in contrast with transitory events« (ibid: 198) they function as a means to domesticate change, to ward off the horrors of contingency that accompany it, and to assign to it the form of a stable, calculable, logically controllable existence.

The question of whether or not force objectively exists might even be wrongly posed in the first place. According to idealist philosophy, force must not be conceptualized as a matter of natural fact, but rather from the perspective of the subject in its cognitive and sensitive faculties.[6] Friedrich Schelling strongly emphasizes the role of the empirical subject as a conceptual benchmark for the understanding of force. On the one hand, he admits that force, in the singular, is »certainly present«, although »only in our concept«. It is just »force *as such*, not *specific* force«. Specific force, on the other hand, i.e. a particular force among others, with a particular degree measured against the degree of those others, discloses itself only in the experience of the subject: »Force is simply that which affects us. What affects us we call real, and what is real exists only in sensation.« (Schelling 1988: 216) Therefore, according to Schelling, *a* force is existent to the extent that it appears to us, regardless of our opinion on the existence of force *as such*.

However, these understandings of force (mechanical or teleological, analytical or synthetical, objective or subjective) remain based on a fundamental assumption that might not be as self-evident as it appears, namely that force (in the singular or the plural) exists as (or can be traced back to) an individual phenomenon. Newton's third law of motion states that when one body exerts a force upon a second body, the second body simultaneously exerts a force equal in magnitude and opposite in direction upon the first body. But, in addition to the physical, there are also ontological reasons why there cannot only be one force, or power, respectively. Iain Hamilton Grant explains:

> A power is a power only if it is resisted by another. If this is not the case, we would be dealing with a power that is not finite. A power which is not limited, in other words, by its products. If we imagine a power unlimited by any product, what is it that this power does? The answer is: absolutely nothing. So, the

---

6 Immanuel Kant counts force among the pure, but derivative, concepts of understanding (predicables) and thus understands it as a pure form of thinking, which proves necessary as a mediator between the a priori concepts of matter and causality (Kant 1996: 134). At the same time, however, he argues that »we do not a priori have the least concept as to how anything can be changed at all«; this is because this concept »requires knowledge of actual forces – e.g., knowledge of the motive forces, or, which is the same, of certain successive appearances (as motions) indicating such forces – and such knowledge can be given only empirically« (Ibid: 273).

power that does absolutely nothing raises the question: is it a power at all?[7] In other words: to posit power entails that there is at least more than one power. (Grant 2014: from min. 8:50 onwards)

As Grant further elaborates, powers must be even conceived of as infinite. This is because, for conceptual reasons, they cannot exhaust themselves in their finite products: the objects. For, if they *could* fully actualize themselves in the products, and if they *could* entirely transform themselves into objects, then a conceptual distinction between the two would no longer be required: there would only be objects.

Forces are not coincident with the objects they produce. Objects, in turn, are not coincident with (natural) being, as it is comprised of productive forces that necessarily exceed the given in its finite completion, i.e. as it is always becoming. Following this argument, a cosmology of forces must account for a multiplicity, in fact an infinity, of forces that determine and specify each other, without ever bringing one another to a halt, thus reifying each other in the given. In other words, forces must be conceptualized as dynamic fields.

Gilbert Simondon's Ontogenetic Force Fields

It is this understanding of force, developed by 19th century electrodynamics and electromagnetism and central to both the relativity and quantum theories of the 20th, that Gilbert Simondon uses as a model for a particular cosmological approach, which focuses less on the ontological state of things: their being, and more on their ontogenetic process: their becoming. Or rather, he develops an ontology of things, in which becoming is not opposed to but integral to being: an ontology of individuation. Therefore, Simondon considers the concept of the field as a true »gift from the natural sciences for the humanities« (Simondon 2013: 544).

Simondon demonstrates the dynamic systematics of such a field by the following example: there is a magnetic field created by three magnets distributed in space. If one introduces a piece of iron that has been demagnetized beforehand, it immediately takes on a magnetic force, depending on the existent field. But as soon as it is magnetized, it in turn affects the struc-

---

7 Grant here alludes to the example of the vitalist conception of a general *Lebenskraft*.

ture of the field and »becomes the citizen of the Republic of the whole, *as if* it were itself a magnet that *creates* a field« (ibid: 545). Therefore, the role of the element in the field is twofold: on the one hand it is the recipient of the force effects of the field, while on the other hand it comes into play »creatively and actively by changing the lines of force of the field« (ibid: 544). The physical concept of the field thus establishes a reciprocity between the ontological status and the operative modalities between the whole and the element. The individual and the field are not isolable entities, but rather express the fundamental reciprocity of the »totality function« and the »element function« within a field. Furthermore, there is no distinction between active and passive elements in a field, as each element is simultaneously active and passive: each affects and is affected. Ultimately, the sum of these interactions is nothing other than the field itself.

In order to understand the reciprocal relationship between element and field in more (practical) detail, we must consider another example that Simondon places centrally in his theory of individuation: the process of crystallization. This occurs when a crystalline germ meets the individuation field of a super-saturated or super-cooled solution (for example: a basin of ice-cold water). Upon arrival, the germ begins to transform the surrounding solution, layer by layer, into crystalline form. The boundary separating the solid crystal from the liquid solution is thus continuously shifted away from the origin of the process, whereby the crystalline form is passed on from layer to layer (»transduction«) – consequently the crystal grows. To the extent that the already created layer forms both the impulse and the structural model for the formation of the next, Simondon literally refers to the process as »in-formation.« The growth continues until the potential energy of the solution is consumed. It then transforms from a metastable to a merely stable state, and the crystal continues to exist in its identical form.

For Simondon, the individuation theory implied by the physical field concept concludes the old philosophical controversy between Platonic theory of ideas and Aristotelean hylomorphism. These two historically dominant ontologies are united and overcome in the reciprocity of individual (crystalline germ) and field (solution): The solution corresponds to the Aristotelian matter that receives a form. The germ corresponds to the Platonic archetype that imposes itself on the matter. In contrast to the ancient models, however, the energy for the becoming of form – the in-formation – does not come from an entelechy or transcendent idea, but rather from the material solution, while the germ functions merely as a trigger.

For Simondon it is not until the introduction of the field concept in 19th century physics that it becomes possible to consider the ontogenesis of an individual without recourse to a metaphysical principle. In the individuation theory that he derives from it, individual being is conceived of in relation to an ontogenetic milieu, rather than in relation to its principal self-identity as an individual. Furthermore, the field in which it comes to being does not previously rest in static indifference, but rather already possesses the potential energy for its formation, as it rests in a merely metastable equilibrium. This energy is the very – non-metaphysical – cause of the individuation of the being.

However, Simondon does not only propose an understanding of the ontogenesis of an individual in general here. With his concept of in-formation he also accounts for the becoming of specific, empirical forms – a model that can be instructive for the analysis of theatrical performance. Despite Simondon's literal interpretation of the concept of information, which shifts it into the realm of material processes, operatively he understands it in the classical cybernetic sense of control. Cybernetically speaking, the dynamic coupling of germ and solution has the character of a modulation: the form is comparable to a signal that controls a relay without adding energy to the work of the effector. However, the information is understood here neither as structure nor as code, but rather as a tension. Namely, it is the tension of individuation between the informative germ and the informable milieu, and as such it is always emergent:

> The information provides the formula that is followed by individuation, and so the formula could not possibly preexist this individuation. One could say that the information always exists in the present, that it is always contemporary, because it yields the meaning according to which a system is individuated. (Simondon 1992: 311)

In other words, the information is absolutely immanent to the process of individuation. It is in the here and now, without referring to a transcendent realm of ideas, norms or signifiers. Form and matter do exist eventually, or rather retrospectively, but they co-emerge and co-constitute each other in the immanence of the individuation process as conditioned by a dynamic field.

What might follow if we consider a theatrical situation to be a force field, which is constituted, distributed, and organized between all elements of the performance as a whole? Or if we compare such an element with an initially discharged piece of iron, as via its transplantation into this particular situation it is emptied (partly) of the use or symbolic value it otherwise represents in the everyday? Or if we imagine that this piece is (re-)formed as an element of performance along the force lines of the dynamic field stretched out between all the others? What happens if we now understand this (re-)formation as a process of in-formation, as the structure of the element and the potential energy of the field productively entangle and resolve into a form? What then?

In-formative Aesthetics

Simondon's theory of in-formation enters into a productive tension with the concept of performativity. This concept has undergone a process of dissolution of its limits since its original definition in John L. Austin's Speech act theory. It was originally coined to specify a particular set of utterances that do not describe reality (constative utterances), but rather change the reality in which they appear, according to certain conditions of possibility. Deconstructing this theory, Jacques Derrida famously showed that the specifics of performative utterances in fact apply to each and every speech act, if not to language as such. Judith Butler applied the notion of performativity to all kinds of acts, including those beyond the realm of verbal language, thus conflating it with the concept and practice of performance. All of these approaches, however, accept the condition that the performative mediates between an immanent act and a transcendent norm, rule, or law. Austin discusses at length the »felicity conditions« (for declarations, requests, and warnings, respectively), by which a performative utterance can be evaluated, often by using juridical examples. Butler describes a normative matrix, or a grid of rules, that can either be reinforced or subverted through the reiteration/deflection of socially coded acts. Furthermore, these theories presuppose a subject that (more or less) intentionally makes these utterances while being (more or less) aware of the underlying normative structures, which means: a human subject. This subject appears in the performative as the agent initiating and executing the act.

There have been attempts, however, at de-humanizing the concept of the performative. For example, Karen Barad's take on a *Posthumanist Performativity* or a *Queer Performativity* of nature (Barad 2003, 2011) is based on a theory of matter as performative materialization (Barad 2007: 59-66, 207-212). Similarly, one could describe the reciprocal becoming of element and field in Simondon as a performative occurrence or happening. But just as in Barad's work, one must struggle then with the concept of normativity implied in classical theories of performativity. In addition, each and every thing appears as a performative utterance or event, causing the concept to lose its validity as designating a specific feature or set of cases (Hölscher 2018). Furthermore, and more importantly, this is not what Simondon proposes. He instead insists on the in-formative character of the individuation process, i.e. on the becoming of form via the reciprocal enactment of form and matter, individual and field, bearing on the force of the former and the energy of the latter. As this entails a becoming of form through and around the relation of an informative germ on the one side and an energetically metastable and thus informable field on the other, the very term of a *per*-formance would indeed be suitable in this instance. But in performativity theory the prefix ›per-‹, indicating the ›through and around‹, is conceived of as a transcendent normative structure. Yet Simondon's use of the in-formative act does not refer to any transcendent causation or regulation: all forms and matters, all forces and energies involved, meet in the immanence of a (trans-)formation of reality. Ultimately, it is the processual aspect of this ontology that appeals to an aesthetic theory of performance as a distributed interplay of forces. This could be conceived of accordingly as an ›in-formativity aesthetics‹ i.e. an aesthetics that would rather focus on the transduction of form than on its iterative citation.[8]

---

8 Simondon himself drew some aesthetical consequences from this aspect, which are of interest here. He develops them against the backdrop of a fundamental doctrine of *Gestalt* psychology, the law of *Prägnanz*. This law states that human perception reduces objects to their simplest forms and thus perceives things as round, rectangular, or triangular, although they are not. Thus, *Gestalt* psychology idealizes symmetrical forms as well-balanced and therefore good forms. Simondon, on the contrary, maintains that it is precisely the *a*-symmetric and therefore tense relations, that provide an informative system with (aesthetic) quality. This is because an informative process requires energetic insta-

Simondon's theory of individuation can be included among the so-called ›flat ontologies‹, i.e. theories of being that do not ground themselves in strongly hierarchical categorizations of modes of being.[9] However, especially in regards to the application of ontological concepts in performance aesthetics, one also needs to account for the differences between the elements of a theatrical situation. And this account should be able to systematically cover the perspective of a spectator, as this perspective is important, if not vital, to theater. Such an account can be found in Whitehead's cosmology to which we now return in order to conclude. This account is particularly interesting in respect to theater, for it differentiates between modes of being via their respective ways and intensities of »expression«. Furthermore, this cosmology can be conceived of as a systematic synthesis of relationality and processuality, the fundamental principles governing Simondon's individuation theory, with a strong emphasis on the process of realization actual events. A brief sketch of Whitehead's differentiation between physical objects versus plant and animal life shall open a perspective for a further elaboration of the cosmological understanding outlined here.

---

bility, whereas harmonic stability means exhaustion or informational decay. »[O]ne would speak of a tension of form and, to the same extent, of a quality of information, which would be concentration up to the disruptive limit, a meeting of opposites in unity, the existence of an inner field to this information scheme, a certain dimension bringing together aspects or dynamisms usually incompatible with each other. This good form or form rich in potential would be a tense complex, a systematized, concentrated plurality; in language, it would become a semantic organism« (Simondon 2013: 550).

9 Simondon sees the process of individuation at work in all modes of existence, although it assumes specific modal forms in each of them. Its pure physical form is exemplified by the process of crystallization (as described above). In the living, individuation already articulates itself as an *individuation system* characterized by interiority and selfhood. In the psychosocial, there are also *inter*-individual processes at work through which the psychic and the social form each other. A special form of this are human societies, in which a *trans*-individual ethics can be realized. According to Simondon, the physical, the living, the psychosocial, and the transindividual build upon one another, so the former is contained by the latter. Therefore, no clear borders and oppositions between the realms can be formed: their differences are not in kind, but of degree and order; the living, for example, is based on the same individuation process as the physical, but here it is more pronounced and reflexively turned towards itself (Simondon 2013).

Conclusion: Expressive Entities in Whitehead's Cosmology

Unlike Simondon Whitehead uses »experience« rather than »individuation« to signify the fundamental ontogenetic process of things. He applies the term in a generic sense including all activities related to the existence of an entity. This »actual entity« is referred to synonymously as an »actual occasion«. This peculiarity speaks to the fact that Whitehead ultimately thinks of entities as events, for they have no existence beyond their own appearances within the experience of others, whether human or other. This generic experience is subdivided into active and passive parts, namely »expression« and »feeling«. Expression leads away from the individual, whereas feeling leads towards him. As with the notion of experience, »expression« is used here in the most generic sense, and is not limited to the wilful production of effects. »Expression is the diffusion, in the environment, of something initially entertained in the experience of the expressor. No conscious determination is necessarily involved; only the impulse to diffuse.« (Whitehead 1968: 21) To the extent that this diffusion is perceived by the others, expression is counter-realized in the form of a feeling. The expression of the one is the feeling of the other and vice versa.

However generic, it is this understanding of expression that allows Whitehead to differentiate between modes of being, for they exercise it in different ways and to different degrees. The inanimate objects of physics are only slightly expressive. They of course remain subject to change, but this usually occurs very slowly. The individual articulates itself rather rarely, and the average prevails instead.[10] This is quite different from the biological: here »nothing average adheres«, and expression is »essentially individual« (ibid: 21). This individuality however is organized differently throughout the living world. Plant life consists of a multiplicity of equal and independent individual centers. Its expression grows out of all of its parts simultaneously. These

---

10 Due to the low expressivity of their objects, the general laws of physics apply in many cases. »It is by reason of average expression, and of average reception, that the average activities of merely material bodies are restrained into conformity with the reigning laws of nature.« (Whitehead 1968: 28) But, as soon as one turns to life, these laws lose their explanatory power, because here the average is dominated by the individual. Ironically, it is the generality of its laws that renders an adequate understanding of the living in physics impossible.

can therefore be detached from the body without lethal consequences. On the contrary, animals' centers of experience are subordinated to the authority of a »central leader« of the whole. Furthermore, theses subordinate centers are indissolubly connected through mutual expression and feeling, and hence cannot be amputated without severe consequences. The individuality of the animal is thus reinforced in two dimensions: the horizontal relation of the parts to each other and the vertical relation to the leader. The expressivity of the animal organism is accordingly composed of the expressions of its parts, which it turns into aspects of its expression as a whole. One could even claim that, according to Whitehead's cosmology, the animal essentially *is* its personal expressivity (ibid: 24-26).

Of course, Whitehead also differentiates between humans and animals in this dynamic natural order of experience. Yet while his discussion of the anthropological problems of abstraction, consciousness, and conceptual reflection mainly concern the inner experience – the feeling – of an individual rather than its expression towards others, Simondon proposes a complementary differentiation between organisms and machines, focusing upon their respective modes of operational relationships to themselves and to their environment (Simondon 2017: 29-39, 1992: 304-306, 2007: 270-275). Both approaches could contribute to a further, more detailed elaboration of cosmological system of theater. However, it was not the aim of this essay to develop such a system, but rather to inspire a certain mode of thinking about performances, in respect to both the production and the reception of theater. If this article were to approach anything as a system, it would be the theatrical situation as an assemblage of diverse forces. Not all of these stem from human considerations, decisions, and intentions, but they nonetheless contribute to the aesthetic becoming of performance via the interaction of the partaking entities or, more precisely, through the reciprocity of the »totality function« and the »element function« in a performative field.

Emerging from the theoretical complex of actor-network theory, new materialism and post-humanism, the concept of »agency« has gained greater popularity since the 2000s. It broadened the scope of the humanities, including theater studies, and partially shifted focus from the human to what is rhetorically called »non-human agency«: an agency that does not entail conscious intentions or rational choice. However, the concept arguably cannot hide its anthropological origins. In any case, it presupposes a subject of action: agency entails an agent. In contrast, Simondon's and Whitehead's cosmological theories are based upon a concept of activity that is stretched out between the individuals in a field. It cannot be reduced to either one of these individuals. On the contrary, the individuals are conditioned by the forces that constitute and stratify the field. They are their ever-emerging products. The forces govern their relations – relations, which, in turn, they support and sustain, repeat and deflect, so that neither can be detached without changing the whole field, nor could either maintain their individuality without it. Therefore, these forces are indeed constitutive of reality and transgressive, as Fischer-Lichte claims in her *Performative Aesthetics*, albeit in a far more general and less heroic sense.[11]

Works Cited

Barad, Karen (2003): »Posthumanist Performativity: Toward an Understanding of How Matter Comes to Matter.« *Signs: Journal of Women in Culture and Society* 28/3, pp. 801-831.

Barad, Karen (2007): *Meeting the Universe Halfway. Quantum Physics and the Entanglement of Matter and Meaning*, (Durham and London: Duke University Press).

Barad, Karen (2011): »Nature's Queer Performativity.« *Qui Parle* 19/2, pp. 121-158.

Fischer-Lichte, Erika (2008 [2004]): *The Transformative Power of Performance. A New Aesthetics*, (London and New York: Routledge).

Grant, Iain Hamilton: »End of Nature«, talk at the conference Nature after Nature, Fridericianum Kassel, July 5, 2014 (https://www.youtube.com/watch?v=IyGh1ZXnXpE).

Hölscher, Stefan: »(Re-)Evaluating Performance since 1990.« *Texte zur Kunst* 28/110, pp. 80-90.

Kant, Immanuel (1996 [1781, 1787]): *Critique of Pure Reason*, (Indianapolis: Hackett Publishing Company).

Leibniz, Gottfried Wilhelm (1989 [1695]): »A New System of the Nature and the Communication of Substances, as well as the Union Between the

---

11 I would like to thank Stefan Hölscher and the editors of this volume, Sabine Huschka and Barbara Gronau, for inspiration and discussion.

Soul and the Body.« In: Leroy E. Loemker (ed.): *Gottfried Wilhelm Leibniz: Philosophical Papers and Letters*, (Dordrecht, Boston and London: Kluver Academic Publishers), pp. 453-461.

Leibniz, Gottfried Wilhelm (1991 [1714]): »Monadology.« In: Nicholas Rescher (ed.): *G.W. Leibniz's Mondaology*, (Pittsburg: University of Pittsburg Press), pp. 45-308.

Menke, Christoph (2013a [2008]): *Force. A Fundamental Concept of Aesthetic Anthropology*, (New York: Fordham University Press).

Menke, Christoph (2013b): *Die Kraft der Kunst*, (Berlin: Suhrkamp Verlag).

Schelling, Friedrich Wilhelm Joseph von (1988 [1797, 1803]): *Ideas for a Philosophy of Nature*, (Cambridge: Cambridge University Press).

Simondon, Gilbert (1992 [1964]): »The Genesis of the Individual. Incorporations.« In: Jonathan Crary/Sanford Kwinter (eds.): *Incorporations*, (New York: Zone Books), pp. 297-319.

Simondon, Gilbert (2007 [1989]): *L'individuation psychique et collective*, (Paris: Aubier).

Simondon, Gilbert (2013 [1958]): *L'individuation à la lumière des notions de forme et d'information*, (Grenoble: Millon).

Simondon, Gilbert (2017 [1958]): *On the Mode of Existence of Technical Objects*, (Minneapolis: Univocal).

Whitehead, Alfred North (1948 [1925]): *Science and the Modern World*, (New York: Pelican Mentor Books).

Whitehead, Alfred North (1967 [1933]): *Adventures of Ideas*, (New York: The Free Press).

Whitehead, Alfred North (1968 [1938]): *Modes of Thought*, (New York: The Free Press).

Whitehead, Alfred North (1978 [1929]): *Process and Reality. An Essay in Cosmology*, (New York: The Free Press).

Forces in Transgression

Gesture, Energy, Critique
Robert Longo and Boris Charmatz

Lucia Ruprecht

If this volume inquires into the potential of energetic forces to become aesthetic interventions, my contribution is based on an understanding of gesture as an aesthetic intervention into energetic force. This understanding is informed by a modernist perspective, which links gesture to the rhythm of intermittency. Within the modernist framework, gestures are energetic phenomena in as much as they are defined by a dialectic between movement and stillness, between kinetic energy and stored, potential energy. It is this particular dialectic that brings about their aesthetic, critical, and political potential, which is accomplished not least by punctuating movement with transitory postural moments of pronounced expressive power. In Walter Benjamin's reading of Bertolt Brecht, gesture is *defined by interruption*: in order to gain shape, gesture temporarily intermits movement flow. »Epic theater is a gestic theater,« writes Benjamin, and he adds »[t]he more frequently we interrupt someone engaged in acting, the more gestures result. The interruption of an action is thus at the foreground of epic theater« (Benjamin 1991: 521).[1] Interruption is to be understood as a de-familiarizing theatrical intervention into everyday gestural regimes, bringing them to a halt and dissecting them in order to reveal their ideological implications. If Brecht and Benjamin formed »one of the classic literary partnerships of the revolutionary Socialist movement« (Mitchell 1998: vii), they also shared a belief in the critical power of a theater that lays bare its own gestural devices, and discloses how these gestural devices reflect back upon the political dimension of social conduct. This momentary interruption, for Benjamin, constitutes not only gesture's condition of emergence, but also its critical agency. It allows

---

1 My translation.

for potentially »messianic arrest[s] of happening,« for brief, vibrating intervals of exposure that enable philosophical or political insight, and which also
provide a »revolutionary chance« (Benjamin 2006: 396).[2]

For the purpose of the following analysis, I define gesture as *movement
that is marked so that it becomes available for expression and reflection.*[3] This
marking is temporal and spatial, and, to varying degrees, semantic. While
my definition of gesture is inspired by modernist thinking, the examples
that I address here are not themselves modernist. Instead I juxtapose Robert
Longo's c. 1980 *Men in the Cities* series of oversized drawings of bodies in
energetic convulsion with Boris Charmatz's 2017 dance piece *10000 Gestures*.
The insights offered by this slightly »disjunctive alignment« (Ngai 2005: 8)
cast light on the theoretical force field that emerges between the parameters
of gesture, energy, and critique. At times, as in *10000 Gestures*, the gestural
body almost bursts with referential associations; at other times, as in *Men
in the Cities*, its prime purpose seems to be its ability to render energy's
mobilization of movement visible. Longo's drawings seek to establish a
moment of high impact, which he calls »that jerking into now« (2015: 7) within
the onceness of the energetic pose. Charmatz multiplies such onceness in
the refusal of repetition. His *10000 Gestures* rejects recursive choreographic
patterns by creating an explosion of singular gestures or moves, which
are carried out by 24 dancers in equally singular sequences. Radically
transient gestures, performed simultaneously, give way to an impression of
permanence and to gestures that seem to be always already there, suspended
in time. As Charmatz writes on his piece: »the chaos of expenditure is so
perfect that it verges on immobility« (Charmatz 2017).[4]

A juxtaposition of *Men in the Cities* and *10000 Gestures*, then, yields insights into questions of choreographed gestural energy. It also enables me to
tease out nuances of gestural political critique in the 1980s and the contemporary period, respectively. This occurs at a time when *avant-garde* concepts
of revolution, such as those of Benjamin and Brecht, have become obsolete.
Men in the Cities stages a ›Punk‹ version of the world of corporate finance by

---

2 See Ruprecht 2015.

3 For an extensive discussion of this definition with reference to modernist dance and cultural theory, see Ruprecht 2019.

4 The non-recursiveness of *10000 Gestures* turns the idea behind Charmatz's 2010 *Levée des
conflits* on its head. In *Levée*, 24 dancers perform the same 25 movements in a potentially
infinite loop.

showing sharply dressed »Wall Street« (Longo 2015: 9) bodies undergoing violent contortions. *10000 Gestures* derives its critical energy from a frantic type of gesturality, which is staged in such excessive variety and acceleration that it causes gestural stress. In Charmatz's piece, gestures are no longer (modernist) aesthetic interventions into energetic force, making this force more expressive, or freezing it in (postmodernist) still frames, as in Longo's work. I contend that Charmatz's gestures can be understood as energetic and expressive force in incessant motion, standing in for the »frenetic negotiations of our busy-bodies« – to cite Eric Santner (2016: 81) – which navigate everyday life in the neoliberal situation. My reading of Charmatz is thus concerned with a form of expenditure of energy that remains ambivalent, wherein the subject constantly feeds an imperative of gestural productivity that is self-perpetuating.

To return to one of the guiding questions of this volume, namely: »how do energetic forces emerge as aesthetic interventions,« Benjamin's modernist answer would be: through modulation and intermittency. These do not imply an absence of energy but rather its temporary storage, so that the thrust of this energy might be transformed, perhaps rerouted, or in a more revolutionary scenario, so that it might be eventually unleashed. This is, in fact, what Longo's monumental images – as monuments dedicated to energetic force – might ultimately intimate. Longo exhibits energy at the instant of its highest concentration.[5] A New York-based visual artist who began to experiment with performance art, sculpture, installations, photography, and video in the 1970s, he increasingly focused on hyper-realistic drawings during and after the 1980s.

Men in the Cities gives evidence of this transition into drawing, but it also encapsulates the decisive influence of other media and physical performance upon the finished work. The initiating impulse for the series was a still from the final scene of Rainer Werner Fassbinder's 1970 film *The American Soldier*, where two gangsters (one of them played by Fassbinder himself) are shot.[6] This scene is a small choreo-affective masterpiece in itself, which transforms into slow motion with the impact of the bullets, to launch into a hyper-extended

---

5 These instants also include narrative aspects; they seem to conjure up cinematic sequences, suggesting narratives that begin before and continue after the captured moment (cf. Dika 2012: 131-133).

6 Clips of the final scene are available on YouTube: https://www.youtube.com/watch?v=L-H2Z5zfwzls (October 12, 2018).

approximately five-minute long sequence in which the gangsters falter, fall, and die. One is cradled by his brother in an abandoned embrace. The sequence is accompanied by a melancholic song about lost love, written by Fassbinder and performed by Günther Kaufmann, who was for a time romantically involved with the director. The filmmaker not only denaturalizes violence by slowing it down, but also bestows an elegiac, erotic and caring duration upon the moment of death. Fassbinder's »anti-naturalist« aesthetic is both »neo-Brechtian« (Webber 2017: 29) and melodramatic. Longo's treatment of Fassbinder's material adds further distance between these layers. Taking a still from the very beginning of the sequence, just before the two men tumble over, he transformed it first into a relief of one of the actors, then a drawing, and finally used it as the inspiration for staging his own choreographic sequences on the rooftop of his studio, asking friends to act as his models. From the resulting photographic material, he produced the meticulous drawings that constitute the *Men* – and women – *in the Cities* series.

This corpus of work is gestural in that it focuses on the interruption of energetic flow, which renders the body energetically, rather than semantically, expressive (see fig. 1). If I define gesture as a movement marked so as to become available for expression and reflection, then energy and its impact on the body become both what is expressed and that which lends itself to be reflected upon in Longo. Energy is a force that hits and thereby provokes gestural and postural reactions from its target. This is demonstrated during the shooting scene that initiated *Men in the Cities*, but Longo further expands on this subtext, explaining that at the time during which he worked on the series, »violence in film was replacing dance or sports« (2015: 7-8) for him. Regarding his photographic sessions, he writes:

> I counted off one, two, three, and the models would have to jerk, fling, twist, fall. Sometimes I'd pick a specific place on the body to throw something at as if they were getting shot in the shoulder or somewhere. (Ibid: 8)

Bodies are ›hit to life‹ by a missile, which in actual fact might just as well transport them to death. The closing sequence of *The American Soldier* spells out this ambivalence between an enhanced kind of physical aliveness and the throes of agony. It also tinges it with gay melancholia, as the film's most emotional physical scene happens between men, as a reaction to the shooting that kills two of the performers.[7] Longo's high-energy moments thus develop around a core of death, connecting the rhythm of temporary pauses arising out of a dialectic of movement and stillness to instances of permanent halt in the extinction of life. In contrast to Fassbinder's film, however, Longo's drawings take movement induced by violence out of its context, thus exhibiting it for a less affectively charged kind of contemplation. Frédéric Pouillaude describes a similar strategy in a recent dance piece on the Israeli occupation by the choreographer Arkadi Zaides, entitled *Archive*.[8] In an analogy to what we understand by »verbatim« quotation, Pouillaude coins the felicitous term »gestuatim« for Zaides' pantomimic copying of moves of physical violence that are projected on the back wall of the stage. Watching these motions taken out of their original context allows us, he writes:

> to see ›more‹: to see the movements for what they are in themselves and not only for the part they play in the world, to perceive their inherent violence, their postural and dynamic similarities, and finally to detect the recurrence of a body image so that, beyond the singularities, something like a collective body becomes apparent. These are the – mostly austere and negative – powers

7   Cindy Sherman writes on Fassbinder's sequence: »Here I was finally watching the ending, over and over about fifty times, riveted by it, realizing I'd overlooked what must have inspired Robert – not merely the ambiguity of the still figure but the core of that sublime scene. Watching that scene in slow-motion, the character's death becomes choreographic, the split second when the ambivalence and grace of the falling figure is balanced between beauty and horror, caught between still and real time, as if we're witnessing every instant of a man before and after death. Not to mention the emotional over-the-top display of grief by the other male character« (2015: 5).

8   Zaides's work *Archive* premiered at the Festival d'Avignon in 2014. It is based on selected footage that was filmed by volunteers working on a project by the Israeli Information Center for Human Rights in the Occupied Territories, B'Tselem. Since 2007, the organization has distributed video cameras to Palestinians in high conflict areas in the West Bank. As a text on Zaides's website explains, »the project aims to provide an ongoing documentation of human rights violations, and to expose the reality of life under occupation to both the Israeli and the international public. On stage, he [Zaides] examines the bodies of Israelis as they were captured on camera, and focuses on the physical reactions to which they resort in various confrontational situations. The Palestinians remain behind the camera, nevertheless, their movement, voice, and point of view are highly present, determining the viewer's perspective. [...] Zaides extracts and appropriates gestures and voices of fellow Israelis. He identifies with the footage and engages in it, gradually embodying it« (Zaides 2018).

of the *gestuatim*: to make movement *strange* and to make this strangeness the
very site of referential knowledge. (Pouillaude 2016: 89)

Longo's gestural stills display individual moments »at the edge of life« (Dika
2012: 132) that are similarly strange and context-free, thus drawing attention
to their movement interest. At the same time, these individual moments are
resonant of collective experience, and refer to distress from an unspecified
source. In the overall trajectory of Longo's oeuvre around the time of the *Men
in the Cities* series, the latter's energetic stills are succeeded by further variations of arrest. Longo followed his drawings of contorting bodies with ones
of »dead figures, splayed on the ground.« He thereafter »resurrected the figures for the last group of drawings,« entitled *Corporate Wars* and *White Riots*,
»where multiple figures are fighting forever, and there's no sides, no one is
winning. That is where the body of work ended« (Longo 2015: 11). In this last
group, inertia is no longer indicative of death, but of indefinite suspension;
a state that is echoed in many of the postures in the *Men in the Cities* series
where bodies are permanently caught in off-balance postures.

The undecidable ambivalence of Longo's bodies, which are at once hy-
per-animated and death-prone, and the moment of political critique that
they might bear will be discussed in due course. However, when considering their staging in a museum or gallery context, a limiting element of this
critique immediately becomes clear. Figure 1 offers an impression of a 2009
exhibition of the series in the New York Metropolitan Museum of Art.

Figure 1: *The Pictures Generation, 1974-1984,* The Metropolitan Museum of Art, The Henry R. Kravis Wing, The Tisch Galleries, April 21 – August 2, 2009. View of three images by Robert Longo displayed in the entry hall of the Metropolitan Museum. New York, Metropolitan Museum of Art.

In this image, the institutional framework of the Met's entrance hall is so overpowering that it nearly asphyxiates the energetic charge of the images. The architectonic setting draws attention to a staggered ensemble of frames surrounding the drawings, to which rope barriers have been added. The institutional containment almost surpasses the energy in the chosen drawings, especially those of the two men left and right, while the female figure in the middle (the model is Cindy Sherman) seems to both protect herself and imitate her confinement by assuming a cross-legged, face-covering pose. Or is the display in the entrance hall meant to encourage visitors to follow the example of Longo's performers by incorporating less usual movement vocabularies as they themselves walk through the galleries?

Boris Charmatz would certainly welcome this interpretation. His *Musée de la danse* has been in operation since 2009 (the concurrence with Longo's exhibition at the Met is coincidental). It favors embodied choreographic interactions as counter-›museal‹, marginal activities which nonetheless redefine the concept of the museum through their opposition:

> we are seeking to invent a museum which is a new type of public space through and for dance [...] dance, as far as museums are concerned, is [...] a potentially dangerous conceptual tool, something that means taking risks, and is rough. Dancers are not just people-who-skillfully-perform-the-movements-the-artist-has-given-them, the star pupils of an art that at last has come to life. (Charmatz 2014: 50-51)[9]

10000 Gestures has not yet been performed in a traditional museum space, such as the MoMA where, during a series of events called *Three Collective Gestures*, Charmatz introduced his ideas about a dancing museum to the New York audience in 2013 (cf. Nicifero 2014). However, the 2017 piece still constitutes a challenge to the idea of ›musealization‹ itself, whether that idea pertains to the assembly of art collections or to a choreographic drive to preserve and repeat. Charmatz calls *10000 Gestures* a »choreographic antimuseum aiming to explore the means of escaping the instinct and the strategies of preservation at work in the activity of a dancer« (Charmatz 2017). It accomplishes this by demanding its dancers to provide the immense, even exploitative amount of energy required to locate and perform non-recursive patterns of movement (fig. 2).

---

9 Charmatz's short statement asks for explanation and exploration; as it stands, it seems to presuppose, in undialectical fashion, that static artworks might be lifeless by dint of their immobility. Hal Foster questions this association of the museum with the »mausoleum,« which often implies »the performative [...] as an almost automatic good« (Foster 2017: 132-135).

Figure 2: Boris Charmatz, *10000 Gestures*, Mayfield Depot, Manchester, 10 July 2017.

I argued at the beginning of this chapter that *10000 Gestures* confronts viewers with a form of gestural stress. Yet despite this, and although it is often rapid and multifaceted, the piece is neither chaotic nor improvised. Charmatz' long-time collaborator Dimitri Chamblas comments that »[i]t is all entirely fixed choreographically, and you have to be very precise, and switch from one parameter to another extremely fast« (Sulcas 2017). In order to design their gestures (which include both dance moves and, more often, all kinds of gesticulation), the dancers followed various themes. These include, for example: »microscopic movements (raising an eyebrow, flicking fingers), violence, eroticism, dance history, obscenity, and politics.« Chamblas specifies: »At the beginning of the piece are the gestures of doing nothing, but very fast, 25 of them; then 15 movements going backwards, then 55 ›crazy‹ movements, then five rest positions. All of that is about a minute« (ibid).

Yet the score is evident to viewers only once they have this information. In a clip from September 14, 2017 of the piece's Berlin premiere at the Tempelhof airport hangar, the beginning's structure is indeed detectible. However, the order appears to be different, including first ›crazy‹ movements and then backwards movements, while the tempo remains restrained in comparison to the speed that subsequently builds. I attended a performance of

10000 Gestures on March 17, 2018 at Musiktheater im Revier, Gelsenkirchen, where it was performed as part of *Tanzplattform Deutschland*. While it took me a while to pick up any possible organizing principles, I was immediately struck by the initially subdued, later more pronounced sense of fatigue that the piece projects.

The viewer is eased into the work's texture by zooming in, at the start, on a single female dancer, dressed in a red, glitzy, two-piece costume consisting of a puff-sleeved bolero and short skirt, as if she were a circus performer of sorts. This dancer launches into a choreographic sequence characterized by the successive unrolling of what might be called *instances of gesture and movement*, strung together, sometimes as dance, sometimes as gesticulation, sometimes as both. For example, her waving turns into a precisely descending arm movement, or her hands touch her face as if in gesticulation, but following unusual, ornamental patterns. She accompanies her gestural dance with a hummed series of sighs and groans, creating a sense of languid, ongoing exhaustion. The humming accompanies the piece's soundscape, which becomes slowly discernible: Mozart's *Requiem*. After a couple of minutes, she begins to emanate fragmentary phrases, such as: »another one, another one.« She tosses around numbers, beginning with the improbable and already overwhelming figure of 2184, thus alerting the audience to the exorbitant nature of the task of devising 10,000 different gestures. She also breaks into some difficult-to-understand shouts, which anticipate the persistent shouting and screaming that will later accompany the group's gestural exercises once the piece's initial and more playful sense of tiredness has given way to feverish over-exertion (see fig. 2).

This solo concludes when the remaining twenty-three performers run onto the dance floor to begin their gestural tasks, which are mostly carried out by the entire group en masse, and only occasionally by smaller constellations of dancers. Each dancer performs their own unique choreographic trajectory throughout. Apart from sequences of orchestrated running and the occasional large jump, expenditure of energy in *10000 Gestures* is not in the first instance connected to the grand movement scales of athletic dance. Dynamism is nuanced and relatively microscopic elements are also included, such as when the dancers are standing or seating on the floor, engaging in upper-body, arm, hand, head and face movements, or in diffuse, uneven twitching. Energy is expended, often almost unbearably so, in the sheer rapidness of succession and the improbable variety of Charmatz's instances of gesture and movement. This impression is enhanced by the manipulation of a communally created force field of intensity that cyclically swells and subsides throughout the piece's duration. The waxing and waning level of intensity echoes the *Requiem,* in which *crescendi* and *decrescendi* function as prominent dramaturgical principles. It is further accentuated by the volume of the musical accompaniment, which is variously increased and decreased. Although some gestural moves are designed to be either in tune with or in counterpoint to the music, the *Requiem* functions above all »as an atmospheric envelope that co-defines the emotional tonality of the performed movements« (Laermans 2010: 411). Like Longo's work, albeit less violently, Mozart's music draws attention to an »underlying idea of death,« which was important to Charmatz during the creation of the piece, as was »the idea of being fully present [...] Every moment says ›now‹« (Sulcas 2017). But, Charmatz is fully dedicated to the liveness of choreography here, in contrast to Longo's use of mediatization. The choreographer preoccupies himself neither with the energy stored in the image, nor with the quotability of a gestural moment that transverses film, live performance, photography, relief, and drawing. *10000 Gestures* is instead explicitly anti-quotable: it confronts viewers with many degrees of stored, potential and kinetically realized energy in ever-changing, more-or-less static, and more-or-less dynamic postures and motions. The piece plays with the idea of dance's ephemerality, and drives this idea to the limits of its radical transience (cf. Sulcas 2017). Longo sought peak energy levels by focusing on postural presence, potentially to the cusp of death; in each of his portraits he aimed to create »an image that happens every time you look at it« (Longo 2015: 11). *10000 Gestures* extends this endeavor to a philosophical comment on the ontology of dance. It insists on the irretrievability of the once-performed and then forever-gone gesture. *10000 Gestures* keeps propelling its instances of gesture and movement. Its logic of irretrievability gives rise to infinite exertion, even during moments of rest where motion is reduced to a minimum, and despite its decreased speed as it concludes.

What should viewers make of the piece's freneticism, its gestural stress in combination with a profoundly liturgical piece of music? This stress takes shape in a massive performance of busy-ness or busy-body-ness, to use Santner's terms (see 2016: 81). Despite its non-business-like costumes, *10000 Gestures* thus resonates with what Longo called corporate wars in the 1980s. Longo's animated agony of white collar office workers stages a revolution in style; or a revolution in style *only*. Its postmodern political critique at once rests in, and is cancelled out by, its self-aware consumerist appeal: his bodies do not sweat.[10] In contrast, in *10000 Gestures* physical effort is tangible. It still seems misleading to connect the piece's spirit of extreme toil to an aesthetic of straightforward political transgression. According to Charmatz's *Undertraining*, which emerged from conversations between him and Isabelle Launay in 2003, »acts of transgression, subversion and disobedience are rare indeed, hence the appeal of the so-called *avant-garde* movements of the 1920s and 30s or the 1960s and 70s« (2011: 16). But Charmatz also voices his reservations about »the endless quest for subversion and transgression« (2011: 24) that we might find in approaches which still consider themselves avant-garde. The »view on the possible forms a show might take« must therefore remain »sceptical«; but this »is coupled with a genuine conviction as to our ability to mobilise forces, to clasp hold of the real, to seize upon things, to jeopardise part of our status, our identity even, within the context of a project exceeding all its actors« (ibid: 16).

10000 Gestures in fact mobilizes and feeds the forces that we love to criticize. It exposes its own hyper-intensity, whether in passages of frantic movement or in moments of intermittent arrest. Its imperative of constant gestural labor is reminiscent of the »24/7 regime of neoliberal capitalism« (2016: 36). Like Charmatz's choice of music, Santner too associates this with a liturgical dimension, which he detects in the afterlife of political theology in secular modernity. This is particularly articulated in Santner's *The Royal Remains* and *The Weight of all Flesh*, which draw upon the issues of splendor and power explored in Giorgio Agamben's *The Kingdom and the Glory*. Santner's work suggests »a new understanding of the irrational core at the center of economic busyness today,« arguing that the »frenetic negotiations of our busy-bodies continue and translate into the doxology of everyday life the liturgical labor that once sustained the sovereign's glory« (Santner 2016).[11] What is implied, here, is that the liturgical work of adoration that once ad-

---

10 In contrast to the perfect drawings, the series of photographs that led to *Men in the Cities* retains more roughness, echoing the roughness that Charmatz in his above-quoted statement on the dancing museum attributes to contemporary dance. The photographs for *Men in the Cities* are reproduced in Longo 2015.

11 This quote refers to the blurb on the back cover. Santner defines doxology as »the ritual praise and glorification of God that constitutes so much of the cultic activity of the Church« (2016: 95). For a fuller discussion of Santner in relation to gestural work, see Ruprecht 2019.

dressed and acclaimed the body of the king has now become dispersed into the »ostensibly secularized, disenchanted locations« (Santner 2011: 245) of political economy.

We have arrived at a state of gesturality where »what matters is not mean-ing-making, but ›who is the master‹ (Deleuze 1990: 18)«, as André Lepecki argues when describing choreography as a performative practice of scoring (2016: 16). What also matters is how well the master is entertained. Many of Charmatz's dancers in *10000 Gestures* are dressed like acrobats or jesters in a non-existent court. If *10000 Gestures* »seizes upon« (Santner 2011: 5) the libidinally driven and secular liturgy of labor, the site of the royal master must remain empty; an emptiness that is disavowed, at great expense, in the agitation of Charmatz's force field of energetic expenditure. Whose orders are they following, and for whom are they delivering their gestural perfor-mance? After the death of the king, the now »sovereign People« are still in »ceaseless motion«, responding to »the imperative of capital accumulation« (Santner 2016: 86). Mozart's music draws attention to this metaphorically liturgical dimension of modern work. But its transcendent power also acts upon the spectacle in a more literal way, as a prayer for eternal rest hovering above a glorious display of undeadness: *Requiem aeternam dona eis, Domine.* In my reading of Longo, I used the term indefinite suspension, which is a state of being that also affects *10000 Gestures*: »It's as if we keep running, the piece will hold together« (Sulcas 2017) Charmatz comments, apparently eliminating any critical impulse that might challenge the cruel necessity of motion.

Michel Foucault famously defines critique as »the art of not being gov-erned quite so much« (Foucault 2007: 45). This 1977 argument does not deny or oppose government, but shifts focus away from legislation imposed by an authority and towards acts of self-legislation. In contrast, Charmatz's piece sometimes creates the impression of dancers in the thralls of remote con-trol. As the work's description for the 2017 Paris *Festival d'automne* states, the dancers seem to be »subject to the laws acting upon them, a pure succession of states and variations of intensity.«[12] If there is critique in *10000 Gestures*, it must operate in and through subjection. Charmatz indeed suggests forms of intervention in contemporary art, which do not simply aim to destroy the

---

12 »Boris Charmatz, 10000 Gestures,« September 7, 2018 (https://www.festival-automne. com/en/edition-2017/boris-charmatz-10000-gestes).

»obstacles« that they target, but »take time to observe them, handle them, take an interest in their origins« (2011: 25). In *10000 Gestures*, such a critical intervention resides in gesturally ›handling‹ the spell of relentless creativity and productivity in neoliberal capitalism. Directing energetic expenditure against its own tyrannical core, it operates »by implosion« (ibid) one might add, using a term that Charmatz applies to contemporary strategies of countering oppression.[13] The wish, and the art, of »not being governed so much« might then arise out of a relentless establishment of total, if diverse, gestural governance.

The imperative of constant gestural work thus collapses in upon itself. Under the heading »Energy« in *Undertraining*, Charmatz states: »With dance, there is something appealing about the very idea of expending energy. It suggests something along the lines of an energy first given, then thrown away, without producing stable objects or, put differently, something that gives off non-capitalisable heat.« (Ibid: 132) Theodor Adorno calls this »over-accumulation,« or the amassing of »excessive and therefore unusable capital« (1967: 177). It is as if *10000 Gestures's* dancers, via their (almost) unstoppable production of non-capitalizable gestural work, deflate the monster that drives them by puffing it up without fail.

Works Cited

Adorno, Theodor (1967): *Prisms*, Samuel and Shierry Weber (trans.), (Cambridge, Massachusetts: The MIT Press).

Agamben, Giorgio (2011): *The Kingdom and the Glory: For a Theological Genealogy of Economy and Government*, (Stanford: Stanford University Press).

Benjamin, Walter (1991): »Was ist das epische Theater? (I).« In: *Gesammelte Schriften*, 7 vols (Frankfurt a.M.: Suhrkamp), vol. II part 2, pp. 519-531.

13 Compare Lepecki's definition of the critical agency of contemporary dance, which he puts in energetic terms: dance generates »charged and vital problematic fields on which pressing and urgent political, corporeal, affective, and social problems are made visible and gather – not to find a solution, but to further the movement of problematization« (2016: 8). Compare also Hal Foster's description of a contemporary, non-heroic avant-garde: »it does not pretend that it can break absolutely with the old order or found a new one; instead it seeks to trace fractures that already exist within the given order, to pressure them further, even to activate them somehow« (2017: 4).

Benjamin, Walter (2006): »On the Concept of History.« In: Howard Eiland and Michael W. Jennings (eds.): *Selected Writings*, Rodney Livingstone (trans.), 4 vols, (Cambridge, Mass.: The Belknap Press of Harvard University Press), vol. 4, pp. 389-400.

Charmatz, Boris/ Launay, Isabelle (2011): *Undertraining: On a Contemporary Dance*, English ed., (Dijon: Presses Du Réel).

Charmatz, Boris (2014): »Interview«, *Dance Research Journal* 46/3, pp. 49-52.

Charmatz, Boris (2017): »10000 Gestures, Choreography: Boris Charmatz«, September 7, 2018 (www.borischarmatz.org/?10000-gestures).

»Boris Charmatz, 10000 Gestures,« accessed September 7, 2018 (https://www.festival-automne.com/en/edition-2017/boris-charmatz-10000-gestes).

Deleuze, Gilles (1990): *The Logic of Sense: European Perspectives*, (New York: Columbia University Press).

Dika, Vera (2012): *The (Moving) Pictures Generation: The Cinematic Impulse in Downtown New York Art and Film*, (New York: Palgrave Macmillan).

Foster, Hal ([2015] 2017): *Bad New Days: Art, Criticism, Emergency*, (London: Verso).

Foucault, Michel ([1997] 2007): »What is Critique?« In: Sylvère Lotringer (ed.), *The Politics of Truth*, Lysa Hochroth and Catherine Porter (trans.), (Los Angeles: semiotext(e)), pp. 41-81.

Laermans, Rudi (2010): »Impure Gestures Towards ›Choreography in General‹: Re/Presenting Flemish Contemporary Dance, 1982-2010«, *Contemporary Theatre Review* 20/4, pp. 405-415.

Lepecki, André (2016): *Singularities: Dance in the Age of Performance*, (New York: Routledge).

Longo, Robert ([1987] 2015): »Interview with Richard Price.« In: Cindy Sherman/Richard Price, *Robert Longo, Men in the Cities: Photographs 1976-1982*, (Munich: Schirmer/Mosel), pp. 7-12.

Mitchell, Stanley (1998): »Introduction.« In: *Walter Benjamin: Understanding Brecht*, (London: Verso, 1998), pp. vii–xix.

Ngai, Sianne (2005): *Ugly Feelings*, (Cambridge, Mass: Harvard University Press).

Nicifero, Alessandra (2014): »OCCUPY MoMA: The (Risks and) Potentials of a Musée de la danse!« *Dance Research Journal* 46/3, pp. 32-44.

Pouillaude, Frédéric (2016): »Dance as Documentary: Conflictual Images in the Choreographic Mirror (On Archive by Arkadi Zaides)«, *Dance Research Journal* 48/2, pp. 80-94.

Ruprecht, Lucia (2015): »Gesture, Interruption, Vibration: Rethinking Early Twentieth-Century Gestural Theory and Practice in Walter Benjamin, Rudolf von Laban and Mary Wigman«, *Dance Research Journal* 47/2, pp. 23-42.

Ruprecht, Lucia (2019): *Gestural Imaginaries: Dance and Cultural Theory in the Early Twentieth Century*, (New York: Oxford University Press).

Santner, Eric (2011): *The Royal Remains: The People's Two Bodies and the Endgames of Sovereignty*, (Chicago: The University of Chicago Press).

Santner, Eric (2016): *The Weight of All Flesh: On the Subject-Matter of Political Economy*, (New York: Oxford University Press).

Sherman, Cindy (2015): »Introduction.« In: Cindy Sherman/Richard Price, *Robert Longo, Men in the Cities: Photographs 1976-1982*, (Munich: Schirmer/Mosel), pp. 5-6.

Sulcas, Roslyn (2017): »A French Choreographer who Plays with the DNA of Dance.« In: *The New York Times*, July 4, 2017, accessed September 11, 2018 (https://www.nytimes.com/2017/07/04/arts/dance/boris-charmatz-a-french-choreographer-who-plays-with-the-dna-of-dance.html).

Webber, Andrew (2017): »The Stylist«, *Sight & Sound* 27/5, p. 29.

Zaides, Arkadi (2018): »Archive«, October 7, 2018 (http://arkadizaides.com/archive).

Training Neoliberal Dancers
Metatechniques and Marketability

Meghan Quinlan

Young dancers approaching college and careers today are confronted with frequent questions about the viability of pursuing their passion full-time from parents, peers, and societal pressures to pursue economically stable pathways. Why major in dance? Why delay college to seek performance opportunities? What can one DO as a dancer? Is this a viable profession? What work has to be done to be successful? Rather than engaging in conversations about the innate importance of performance, corporeal innovation, and movement, such questions often prompt discussions about the economics of dancing in the contemporary moment.

The issue of contemporary dance training that results in professional (paid) opportunities to dance has been the subject of a seven-year ethnographic research project focusing on the practice of Gaga: an improvisatory dance method developed by Israeli choreographer Ohad Naharin in the early 2000s. The population that I have studied throughout my research is primarily American and European dancers between eighteen to twenty-five years old, with interest in joining companies whose style is similar to the aesthetic of Batsheva or other technically demanding groups that utilize improvisation and physical extremes. This is the dominant population of Gaga/dancer participants but does not cover the full scope of Gaga/dancer and Gaga/people class attendance. Thus, what I propose in this chapter is a critical reading of the dominant utilization of Gaga by aspiring dance professionals in the concert dance world from an American perspective rather than a definitive analysis of Gaga across all cultures and contexts. In studying this popular dance training trend, I utilize ethnographic, analytic, and phenomenological perspectives to consider what skills the aspiring dancer today has to master to be competitive in the contemporary dance performance market in the early 21st century.

In the contemporary moment, dancers are expected to be thinking movers rather than rote technicians. As noted by dance scholars such as Susan Foster (2010) and Melanie Bales and Rebecca Nettl-Fiol (2008), since the turn of the 21st century there has been a shift in training trends away from pure mimicry of form and toward an increased emphasis on developing metacognitive approaches to creating movement. While any class intended to improve one's skill as a dancer is often colloquially referred to as a »technique« class, I suggest that there are multiple approaches to »technique« being utilized in dance classrooms across various genres of movement, some of which stray from the conventional understanding of form-based techniques. Metatechniques, for instance, are teaching strategies to negotiate movement invention and performance as a choice-making progress rather than an enforced form to be copied.

A key example of what I refer to as a metatechnique, or a metacognitive approach to teaching movement invention and performance, is the emerging trend of Gaga. Now the training method of the Tel Aviv-based Batsheva Dance Company, Gaga became internationally popular alongside Batsheva's performances during Ohad Naharin's tenure as Artistic Director of the company (1990-2018). The practice of Gaga, named as such, is new. Yet many of the concepts behind its practice, such as manipulating the effort, shapes, and intents of dancers imbued with personal agency beyond the performance of pre-choreographed movement, are mainstays in the modern and contemporary dance historical continuum as well as other contemporary practices such as Countertechnique and Body Weather.[1] In this chapter, I offer a brief analysis of the structure of Gaga classes to understand the ways in which this contemporary practice addresses issues that are common to dance markets over time, yet particularly suited to the emergence of the neoliberal dance market that requires dancers to be physically, emotionally, and

---

1 Countertechnique is a dance practice created by Anouk Van Dijk, who is currently Artistic Director of the company Chunky Move in Australia. Body Weather is an approach to movement invention developed by Japanese dancer Min Tanaka on a farm in Japan between 1985-2010. There are many other choreographers and dancers developing similarly metacognitive approaches to movement and improvisation that reject the primacy of form to instruct movement, such as the recent development of Fighting Monkey Practice by Linda Kapetanea and Jozef Frucek.

mentally flexible and innovative by blurring the pedagogical norms of teaching technique, choreography, and improvisation.

This mix of approaches used in Gaga is what I would describe as a »metatechnique«, or a metacognitive method of movement invention. I refer to the origin of this term that comes from the analysis of the agency of a dancer by Randy Martin, who argued that dancers maintain individual agency even while working for a choreographer because the dancer's internal negotiation of bodily training and technique are necessary to learn and execute choreography. He wrote in 1998 that »choreography is a metatechnique. It is a method for generating means of movement [offering] a basis for differentiating movement values out of a given cultural context that provides the orienting principles for a body of techniques« (Martin 1998: 214). This definition accurately describes what Gaga and many other contemporary training methods do: teach students strategies for differentiating movement qualities and forms, and develop strategies for drawing on and orienting the multiple techniques that dancers bring with them to the Gaga classroom. This definition also prompts an analysis of Gaga in its cultural and economic context to better understand its orienting principles for movement, which is a perspective that is largely missing in existing literature on Gaga (Katan 2016, Galili 2015) but integral to understanding the motivations behind shifts in training practices that are not due solely to artistic innovation.

Technique

In the process of researching Gaga, I have frequently interviewed dancers who refer to Gaga as a »technique«. In spite of this recurring colloquial use of the term to describe Gaga, it is a label that Ohad Naharin actively rejects. In an open question and answer session during the 2015 Gaga Summer Intensive in Tel Aviv, I asked Naharin why he calls Gaga a movement language and how that separates the practice from techniques or other somatic practices. He answered simply:

> Well, before I called Gaga »Gaga«, I called it my movement language. So, it's not that I call Gaga my movement language; my movement language is called Gaga. And the reason it's my movement language, and not a technique, is because I feel that by calling it a movement language, it stays open

for changes ... A technique it feels like something more finished. Done. That's it. (Unpublished interview with author)

Naharin's perception of what a technique is – fixed – provides his justification for refusing to ascribe this label to Gaga. Indeed, this understanding of technique is a common one because of the prevalence of modernist techniques designed by and named after individual choreographers and remaining largely unchanged over time (i.e. Graham, Horton, Humphrey, Laban, Cunningham).

Classifying Gaga as a movement language rather than as a technique consciously attempts to dissociate the practice from the concert dance world, which relies heavily on the mastery of specific techniques. Dismissing the idea of Gaga as a technique also rhetorically distances the practice from the cultural and racial hierarchies so commonly associated with the term and theoretically invites a range of movements regardless of aesthetic or cultural background. Yet, the prevalence of Europeanist techniques within the practice of Gaga challenges the viability of denying Gaga's association with both the pedagogical structure of form-based techniques and the sociopolitical histories of the term, which at least in the American understanding are deeply rooted in racist and classist hierarchies.[2]

The trend of choreographers naming techniques after themselves to codify their personal choreographic and aesthetic preferences during the modern period of American dance history in the 20th century further solidified this colloquial understanding of techniques as static, form-based practices with clear top-down power dynamics between a teacher and a group of students. This type of class structure, which is still common in many forms of dance training today, was examined by Susan Foster in the seminal article »Dancing Bodies« (1997), where she analyzed the process of learning a form-based technique through perception, mimicry, and idealization. In it, she suggests that techniques aim at »creating the body« of a particular dancer to adhere to a unified aesthetic, using case studies such as ballet, Cunningham technique, and contact improvisation to illustrate the ways that the process-

---

2 The issues of race and class embedded in the practice of Gaga are further explored in other publications by the author, and track aesthetic as well as institutional and rhetorical links to American modern dance practices and their histories of racist and classist segregation (Quinlan 2016a, 2016b).

es can shift to form bodies for these particular practices. Foster presents the agency of the dancer required to successfully move through this type of technical training as rooted in the internal process of interpreting and adapting external visual and verbal cues into one's own body. At the same time, the dominant powers in the classroom are that of the teacher and the ideal of the form that students strive to reach.

The same process of learning a technique is unpacked by Martin in his chapter »Between Technique and the State« (Martin 1998). He suggests that technique can serve a function of the state and thus act as a coercive power training bodies to be subservient to an authoritarian power, much like Foucault's theory of docile bodies (Foucault [1977] 1995). Martin also acknowledges that in the process of learning a specific dance technique, one has to contend with a range of techniques already residing in the body. He suggests that:

> The prospect that contending principles of movement reside within the same body suggests that part of the effort entailed in learning a technique has to do with the dancer's ability to generate terms of mediation among different demands on the body. In this process of self-governance, a technique for regulating techniques, the dancer must generate her own authority. (Martin 1998: 175)

While this process of self-governance is left to the individual in the case of the modern dance techniques Martin references here, the pedagogical imperative of Gaga challenges the naturalization of this process as teachers provide explicit suggestions to students prompting their approach to shifting between forms, dynamics, and styles of movement. Martin's statements about the agency of the dancer in the context of a Graham technique class do not entirely apply to the improvisational structure of Gaga. While there are similarities between the authoritative teacher in Graham classes (for more on Graham's pedagogy, see Franko 2012, Horosko 2002) and the Gaga teacher leading the improvisational prompts in that they both guide the class's structure, the power ascribed to the teachers in these two instances varies greatly. Even as the Gaga teacher imparts suggestions and models for approaching certain technical skills, such as switching between two dynamics quickly or remaining light during jumps, the student is granted greater freedom for self-exploration within this prompt. Whereas mimicry is an integral component of a strictly form-based technique such as Graham, external mimicry and form is only one component within Gaga. This changes the transfer of knowledge and the power dynamics between teacher and student. Though I would argue that although Gaga classes do impart techniques for forms and encourage mimicry (there is even a Gaga term called kagami that refers to the mirroring process of looking at the teacher to get the essence of what he/she is doing) it is not entirely in line with the usage discussed by Martin.

Students develop a toolbox of metatechnique skills in Gaga classes, practicing a large range of approaches to moving the body. Gaga dancers learn how to embody drastically different dynamics, speeds, textures, levels, and postures and shift between them almost instantaneously; embodying all of these different ways of moving the body is seen as a tool, as is the skill of shifting between them quickly. This toolbox of skills helps dancers expand their range and physical capabilities. Therefore, Gaga does not function as a stand-alone technique like bharata natyam (cf. Kedhar (2014) or ballet, but rather as a method of developing strategies and tools to differentiate between styles and dynamics, in part because of the multiple influences on Naharin's dancing body that became part of Gaga. It is thus the container to hold these tools learned to negotiate the multiple techniques now expected of dancers in the contemporary concert dance market.

I suggest that this technique for regulating techniques that Martin defines as an internal »process of self-governance« is now being taught in Gaga as a metatechnique. Acknowledging Gaga as a technique for regulating techniques suggests that Gaga is itself a technique, although it is not a form-based technique in the conventional modern-dance sense. As a metatechnique focused on how to approach internal negotiations of style and form, the practice of Gaga challenges the idea that these processes of self-choreographing – negotiating bodily techniques within one's body – are *naturally* happening. Acknowledging this conscious labor of internal negotiations of multiple bodily techniques challenges the power dynamics often assumed to exist within the dance classroom by giving increased agency to the dancers as choreographer of their internal processes. The increasing prevalence of dancers having to negotiate multiple techniques within the body has created a fertile space for metatechniques to emerge. These practices offer strategies for self-governance in a way that was perhaps not as crucial when dancers were more often able to stay in one technique rather than being expected to be masters of multiple techniques as is required in the neoliberal market. If this self-governance of techniques within the body is counterhegemonic to the authority of the modern dance instructor, then how does the structure of agency change in the context of a class that is teaching students strategies for self-governance? Does this newfound attention to the process of self-governance and how to control it challenge previous scholarship on the agency of the dancer in modern dance techniques, or contemporary ways of engaging with, learning, observing, or analyzing dance?

Choreography

Similar to the term »technique«, choreography is a label consciously rejected by Naharin to describe the practice of Gaga. This differentiation between Gaga and his personal choreographic practice allows for a critical distance between a practice that is intended for wide distribution and his personal artistic vision that is predicated not on Gaga's principles, but rather his own strategic editing and compositional strategies. When asked about his creative process in a question and answer session during the Summer 2015 Gaga Intensive, Naharin clarified that for his work with the Batsheva Dance Company »Gaga is our toolbox, but Gaga is not choreographing.« He continued to clarify the relationship between Gaga and choreography in response to a question about the difference between Gaga/people and Gaga/dancers: »It's very clear that to dance doesn't mean to perform. Doesn't mean to be on stage. To dance is not about performing, is not about choreography« (Ohad Naharin, July 31, 2015). Naharin suggests here that dancing is an act separate from choreography and that engaging with Gaga is important for everyone regardless of potential interest in performing.

Though Naharin acknowledged that Gaga provided many tools and inspiration for his choreographic works, his statements infer that there is no inherent tie between Gaga practice and performance. Indeed, Gaga is structured as a stand-alone practice. Because it is theoretically not tied to a particular choreographic vision, Gaga is open for students to manipulate and engage with through their own artistic and aesthetic visions.

Although individual choreographers may utilize tools learned in Gaga as part of their own choreographic practices or inspiration, and while students can use skills from Gaga to learn and perform staged works, Gaga itself only exists in a class format. This separation is made explicitly clear through the use of two tracks of Gaga: Gaga/dancers and Gaga/people. The Gaga/people track in particular emphasizes that dancing does not need to be linked to performance; this idea is often carried over into Gaga/dancer classes as well.

Yet, if we understand choreography in a more expansive sense of the term not directly tied to stage performance, we can see how teachers and students in Gaga classes are engaging in choreographic acts. Acknowledging the choreographic component of Gaga, for both teacher and student, complicates the agency ascribed to the student. The students are learning and replicating techniques for creating movement, and the inference is that the students' agency is contingent on their understanding of the authority figure leading the class. Yet, there is also space for students to regain control and choreograph their own experiences by choosing when to apply or ignore the teacher's prompts, thus choreographing their own participation in the class: a skill required of thinking dancers who hope to find employment on the job market.

By applying the definition of choreography in its broadest sense to Gaga – organizing or creating a score for movement – it is clear that Gaga embodies multiple choreographic moments. The teachers choreograph the class by leading the students through a series of tasks, sensations, and guided improvisations. A standardization of Gaga teachers is enforced through regular check-ins in Tel Aviv, and as a result the teachers (of which there are over 130 as of 2018) exhibit very similar ways of introducing prompts. The codification of Gaga is even stronger in Israel, where teachers are required to do more frequent check-ins. Rossi Lamont Walter, an American dancer who moved to Israel to dance for a year, noted that »the language that's used, the images that are used ... each teacher has their sort of favorite, maybe something that resonates for them, but I think the language in Gaga classes feels pretty consistent« (interview with author). This consistency within the language used in Gaga illustrates the uniformity of tools employed by Gaga teachers in the choreography of their individual classes, stemming from Naharin's own research and vision of what Gaga can and should teach students.

At the same time, Walter notes that the teachers demonstrate clear preferences when designing their classes, a fact that resonated in my interviews with Gaga teachers. As a result, students frequently have strong opinions about their favorite instructors. Some students will not take a class with someone they dislike even if they are usually avid Gaga participants. This similarly influences the students' attitudes in class and how they choose to choreograph their own movements and reactions to the teacher's instructions. Though students are frequently urged to let go of their consciousness and not plan movements, relying instead on listening to the body and its sensations, this release of agency to the dancers is often introduced as a method for students to methodically explore existing prompts or movement ideas in multiple ways. Thus, even in their supposed moment of freedom to create, the students' inspiration is supposed to be rooted in the prompts offered by the instructor, potentially limiting the scope of their exploration if they are diligently following all class prompts and engaging with the teacher's choreographed sequence of movement exploration.

Acknowledging the ways in which both teachers and students can choreograph their activity in the classroom brings this chapter back to the question about agency in dance. The recognition of agency often centers on the term »choreography« because this label infers ownership and active control over the creation and structuring of movement (Foster 2011). As Gay Morris and Jens Giersdorf explain:

> Choreography [is] an organizational, decision-making, and analytical system that is always social and political. This incorporates established definitions of choreography as purposeful stagings of structured, embodied movements that aim to communicate an idea or create meaning for an actual, conceptual, or purposefully absent audience for aesthetic and social reasons. Important for this definition is the acknowledgement of training, technique, rehearsal, performance, and reception as intrinsic parts of choreography, not only to reveal labor and agency but also to examine discipline and resistance to it. (Morris and Giersdorf 2016: 7)

Gaga classes are purposefully absent of audiences, to encourage open student investigation by limiting the inhibitions that can arise from having observers present. Yet thinking of Gaga in this choreographic framework, even though it is not rooted in an intent to create a staged choreographic production, allows for an acknowledgment of the politics of labor and agency within the process of taking the class. With the guidance of imagery, sensations, and movement suggestions, the students are required to create, research, and develop their own movement. Although this movement is not intended to be repeated, edited, or performed for an audience, the process of selecting, creating, and placing movement remains present. This happens at a self-choreographic level, referring to the process of negotiating the many techniques within one's body as well as to the choreographing of external forms through solo improvisation. Gaga, as a metatechnique, integrates the practice of choreographing, embodying specific techniques, and improvising movement. Acknowledging the choreographic elements in Gaga, for both the teacher and the student, is critical for recognizing the agency of the dancers to make their own decisions about where, when, and how to move even as they are actively learning techniques for making these decisions and adhering to an instructor's directions.

Improvisation

Gaga classes are not advertised as improvisation; yet, the structure of the class is guided improvisation. Teachers present movement prompts and suggestions that depend on sensations (i.e., taste something good) and imagery (i.e., imagine balls of energy running through the highways of your body) as well as physical forms (i.e., extend your bones into space and make straight lines with your body, as if the bones are breaking through the skin because of the energy of their reach) for the students to explore in their bodies. The teachers introduce suggestions frequently and regularly, giving students just enough time to explore the sensation before being urged to add another task. However, the students are theoretically free to follow or ignore these verbal and physical cues because there is a lack of formal corrections and unity in the class structure. In both Gaga advertising and colloquial conversations with Gaga students, this guided improvisational structure with the onus on the student's in-the-moment choice making is often connected to the »experience of freedom and pleasure« (Gaga Movement Ltd. 2018) that is advertised as being present in Gaga classes. As Danielle Goldman notes: »Such celebratory pairings of improvisation and freedom are common in the field of dance – not only in colleges but also among critics, scholars, and practicing artists across a range of genres.« (Goldman 2010: 1)

Despite the common association with freedom and improvisation, several scholars have begun to denaturalize this concept and assert the labor and limitations of improvised movement. For instance, David Gere points to the cognitive labor in improvisation: »It is while improvising that the body's intelligence manifests itself most ineluctably, and that the fast-moving agile mind becomes a necessity. The body thinks. The mind dances« (Gere 2003: xiv). Goldman argues that movement improvisation always exists in a »tight space« of constraints, and that understanding that »one could escape confinement only to enter into or become aware of another set of strictures is vital to understanding the political power of improvisation« (Goldman 2010: 4). According to this logic, because improvisation exists within a set of constraints and rules, it cannot be inherently free or natural, even though Gaga's advertising continuously appeals to these ideas.

Although Gaga falls into the tropes of connecting improvised dancing to freedom in its advertising rhetoric, the refusal to designate the class as improvisation alone points to the heavy structure embedded in the improvisatory elements of this metatechnique. In an interview Gaga teacher Deborah Friedes Galili described how:

> … sometimes there's confusion about whether Gaga is improvisation, and the place that I'm at in my understanding of it is that we're using improvisation as a tool but Gaga itself is not an improvisation class. Gaga offers some tools which can address some of the goals of a traditional improvisation class … and yet I'm not aiming at that same end point, even though most of the time I am in fact improvising.

Her complication of the label of improvisation is an important distinction for understanding the power dynamics and agency within the Gaga classroom. Though the teachers' prompts are presumably tools to lead participants to the »experience of freedom« advertised on Gaga's homepage, the frequent prompts from instructors consciously restrict the freedom that can be found in Gaga by imposing a great deal of direction on the improvisation. The reminder from a teacher to never stop moving in the middle of an aggressively vigorous jumping exercise certainly does not feel like an invitation to enact your full range of free will, for instance. The verbal cues given by instructors to guide students closer toward a specific physical embodiment of a Gaga concept are also often repeated and rephrased to move toward a specific result. Because Gaga is a class designed to impart metacognitive« skills about choice making, it is not actually an exercise in attempting to find an absolute, idealistic freedom of movement as it is often advertised to be; rather, it is the rehearsal of choice-making strategies imparted by the instructor. Recognizing the ways in which improvisation and the skills required to improvise in different mediums suggest a relationship more akin to technique and the learning of specific skills again returns to Gaga's blurring of these different approaches to movement creation and execution: technique, choreography, and improvisation.

Neoliberalism and Dance in the Twenty-First Century

Gaga is one of the most sought-after training methods for contemporary dancers on the global contemporary dance market, and its focus on improvisation and teaching dancers skills for negotiating multiple stylistic and formal influences falls in line with contemporary demands from popular choreographers such as Hofesh Schechter and Jiri Kylian, as well as from college dance programs such as Juilliard and Harvard. As several dance scholars have documented, choreographers and dance companies in the present have radically changed from the modernist model of a single director/choreographer with a large, semi-stable company of dancers trained to excel in a single technique or style (Bales and Nettl-Fiol 2008; Foster 1997 and 2010; Kedhar 2014). Dancers are now expected to excel in multiple styles rather than specialize in one, and be available for impermanent contract work. This trend, although in part due to changes specific to the dance market, follows neoliberal market trends that demand efficiency, flexibility, and multiple skills from laborers (Brown 2015; Hardt and Negri 2012; Martin 2012; Standing 2011; Harvey 2007; Ong 1999).

The structure of Gaga as a metatechnique falls in line with neoliberal values of efficiency that require laborers to be skilled in multiple rather than specialized tasks.[3] Gaga is a popular training method that teaches danc-

---

3 Neoliberalism, as both an economic practice and a term, emerged in the second half of the twentieth century in South American countries such as Chile and then in several major national economies such as Britain, the United States, and China. Several major economies shifted to free market models led by governments that believed personal and financial freedom comes from a diminishment of government oversight in the market (Brown 2015; Harvey 2007; Hardt and Negri 2012; Martin 2012). Emerging partly out of a reaction against Cold War politics and the threat of communism, neoliberal economic policies move away from government intervention to emphasize deregulation, privatization, and individual entrepreneurial freedom. These shifts were geared toward personal and political freedom for individuals, which was theoretically attainable if individuals had the ability to enter the market and have free will as both workers and

ers skills to excel in this neoliberal model of flexible labor, and better understanding how it is structured and what it teaches students through its metatechnique pedagogical structure offers insights into the socioeconomic impacts of neoliberalism on global dance training and the development and recognition of a dancer's agency. Though Gaga and neoliberalism do not directly mirror one another, there are overwhelming similarities in the guiding principles of both. For instance, both are interested in developing efficient workers and privilege the individual as the primary agent for one's own destiny, even while creating strict structures in which this individuality is allowed to exist (Brown 2015; Harvey 2007; Standing 2011). Even as Gaga resists some neoliberal values, such as the move away from physical labor to the financialization of economies, this metatechnique is able to produce dancers that are prepared to excel in contemporary neoliberal dance economies through the focus on self-negotiating multiple skills. I do not suggest that Gaga's ability to produce dancers well prepared for the current dance market is an intentional reaction to the economic climate, nor is it Naharin's goal for Gaga practice. Yet regardless of whether or not this was the impetus for creating Gaga practice, the fact that it is being utilized as a training tool in the contemporary moment helps one understand the demands placed on dancers today and how Gaga has prepared them for success.

In the current moment, the global concert dance market privileges dancers that are independently motivated, excel at improvisation, and are able to work in flexible pickup jobs: these are all traits of the precariat class that emerged as a result of neoliberal economic trends. Gaga thrives in this context because it consciously develops these qualities of self-direction that dancers must now excel at in order to be marketable. For instance, Meredith Clemons, a recent college graduate training in Europe at the time of our interview explained that she continues doing Gaga because she finds it personally enjoyable but also important for professional development:

> Particularly because lots of choreographers are looking for collaborative
> dancers, and dancers that have improvisation experience, and even though

---

consumers. Significantly, this freedom has not been made available to all workers. Economists such as Guy Standing (2011) and Michael Hardt and Antonio Negri (2012) have argued that these neoliberal policies have produced a class they have termed the precariat, resulting in increased pressure on workers to be flexible in terms of contracts, schedules, and skills.

we talked about that it's actually a quite structured improvisation class, there are those moments, especially as classes get to the end, where you're just given complete freedom to play with the tools you've been given. I think I've become a much better improvisational dancer since starting Gaga, which in today's dance world is I think pretty invaluable when you're looking for work.

The status of dancers seeking a company to join is representative of the growing class of the precariat. Their lack of job security and the need to sell their own labor, rather than the capitalist model of managing one's own means of production to hire other laborers to make a profit, places this class of workers at the mercy of employers. Though this is hardly a new state of affairs in the dance economy (the presence of dance companies able to employ their workers full time has always been limited, and dancers frequently commit to short-term gigs for little or no pay), in the neoliberal market contract work rather than full-time employment has begun to rise in other sectors of the economy as well. The basic skills of negotiating multiple bodily techniques learned in Gaga are similar to the ones necessary to survive in any neoliberal labor market. The recognition that these skills must be learned challenges the inherent agency often ascribed to students in movement practice, but at the same time it points to the importance of students acquiring these skills and the increased mobility and marketability that dancers stand to gain from engaging in metatechniques such as Gaga, an engagement that ultimately gives them more agency in their overall labor experience in the neoliberal framework.

Although Gaga was not intentionally designed to further neoliberal agendas of personal freedom and personal development for economic gain, it can be easily subsumed in this process because of its applicability to contemporary demands in dance markets. This analysis of Gaga may prove useful for understanding the plight of contemporary dance artists and what they must do to remain competitive in today's economic markets, and it also questions the impact that economics can have on artistic practices and pedagogies. If neoliberal economics continue to be a dominant model internationally, thus forcing individuals to remain competitive and economically motivated in all sectors of life, I argue that the pedagogical structures of practices, such as Gaga, that are used by dancers for professional development will remain influenced by the need to make progress for professional development and job security in the contemporary dance market. As long as these neoliberal pressures remain, dance training systems such as Gaga – and the types of agency they encourage and train students to embody – cannot be considered to be devoid of external economic influence. As such, I strongly suggest that the economic pressures placed on Gaga participants reduces their ability to fully engage in the utopian visions presented in class, and this pressure must be acknowledged in light of the advertising rhetoric that attempts to distance Gaga from these realities.

Works Cited

Bales, Melanie/Nettl-Fiol, Rebecca (eds.) (2008): *The Body Eclectic: Evolving Practices in Dance Training*, (Champaign: University of Illinois Press).

Brown, Wendy (2015): *Undoing the Demos: Neoliberalism's Stealth Revolution*, (New York: Zone Books).

Butler, Judith (1993) [2011]: *Bodies That Matter: On the Discursive Limits of Sex*, (London and New York: Routledge).

Foster, Susan Leigh (1997): »Dancing Bodies«. In: Jane C. Desmond (ed.): *Meaning in Motion*, (Durham: Duke University Press), pp. 235-258.

Foster, Susan Leigh (2009): »Choreographies and Choreographers.« In: Susan Leigh Foster (ed.): *Worlding Dance*, (New York: Palgrave Macmillan), pp. 98-118.

Foster, Susan Leigh (2010): »Dancing Bodies: An Addendum, 2009«, *Theater* 40/1: pp. 25-29.

Foster, Susan Leigh (2011): *Choreographing Empathy: Kinesthesia in Performance*, (London and New York: Routledge).

Foucault, Michel (1977) [1995]: *Discipline and Punish: The Birth of the Prison*, Alan Sheriden (trans.), (New York: Vintage Books).

Franko, Mark (2012): *Martha Graham in Love and War: The Life in the Work*, (Oxford and New York: Oxford University Press).

Gaga Movement Ltd. (2016): »Gaga People.Dancers.« Oct 27, 2018 (http://gagapeople.com/english/).

Galili, Deborah Friedes (2015): »Moving Beyond Technique with Ohad Naharin in the Twenty-First Century«, *Dance Chronicle* 32/3, pp. 360-392.

Gere, David (2003): »Introduction.« In: Ann Cooper Albright/David Gere (eds.): *Taken by Surprise: A Dance Improvisation Reader*, (Middletown, CT: Wesleyan University Press), pp. xiii-xxi.

Goldman, Danielle (2010): *I Want to Be Ready: Improvisation as a Practice of Freedom*, (Ann Arbor: University of Michigan Press).

Hardt, Michael/Negri, Antonio (2012): *Declaration*, (Argo-Navis), Kindle edition. Harvey, David (2007): *A Brief History of Neoliberalism*, (New York and London: Oxford University Press).

Horosko, Marian (2002): *Martha Graham: The Evolution of Her Dance Theory and Training*, (Gainesville: University Press of Florida).

Jackson, Jonathan David (2001): »Improvisation in African-American Vernacular Dancing«, *Dance Research Journal* 33/2, pp. 40-53.

Katan, Einav (2016): *Embodied Philosophy in Dance: Gaga and Ohad Naharin's Movement Research*, (New York: Palgrave Macmillan).

Kedhar, Anusha (2014): »Flexibility and Its Bodily Limits: Transnational South Asian Dancers in an Age of Neoliberalism«, *Dance Research Journal* 46/1, pp. 23-40.

Kraut, Anthea (2015): *Choreographing Copyright: Race, Gender, and Intellectual Property Rights in American Dance*, (Oxford and New York: Oxford University Press).

Marks, Victoria (2003): »Against Improvisation: A Postmodernist Makes the Case for Choreography.« In: Ann Cooper Albright/David Gere (eds.): *Taken by Surprise: A Dance Improvisation Reader*, (Middletown, CT: Wesleyan University Press), pp. 135-140.

Martin, Randy (1998): *Critical Moves: Dance Studies in Theory and Politics*, (Durham and London: Duke University Press).

Martin, Randy (2012): »A Precarious Dance, a Derivative Sociality«, *TDR/The Drama Review* 56/4, pp. 62-77.

Mauss, Marcel (1935) [1992]: »Techniques of the Body.« In: Jonathan Crary/Sanford Kwinter (eds.): *Incorporations*, (New York: Zone), pp. 455-477.

Monroe, Raquel (2011): »»I Don't Want to do African . . . What About My Technique?«: Transforming Dancing Places into Spaces in the Academy«, *The Journal of Pan African Studies* 4/6, pp. 38-55.

Morris, Gay/Giersdorf, Jens Richard (2016): »Introduction.« In: Gay Morris/Jens Richard Giersdorf (eds.): *Choreographies of 21st Century Wars*, (New York: Oxford University Press), pp. 1-24.

Novack, Cynthia J. (1990): *Sharing the Dance: Contact Improvisation and American Culture*, (Madison, Wisconsin: University of Wisconsin Press).

Ong, Aihwa (1999): *Flexible Citizenship: The Cultural Logics of Transnationality*, (Durham: Duke University Press).

Ong, Aihwa (2006): *Neoliberalism as Exception: Mutations in Citizenship and Sovereignty*, (Durham: Duke University Press).

Quinlan, Meghan (2016a): »Gaga as Politics: A Case Study of Contemporary Dance Training.« (PhD, University of California, Riverside).

Quinlan, Meghan (2016b): »Abstractions of Whiteness in Downtown Los Angeles: Ate9's *Kelev Lavan*«, *TDR/The Drama Review*, 60/3, pp. 171-7.

Rowe, Nicholas (2009): »Post-Salvagism: Choreography and Its Discontents in the Occupied Palestinian Territories«, *Dance Research Journal* 41/1, pp. 45-68.

Savigliano, Marta (2009): »Worlding Dance and Dancing Out There in the World.« In: Susan Leigh Foster (ed.): *Worlding Dance*, (New York: Palgrave Macmillan), pp. 163-190.

Standing, Guy (2011): *The Precariat: The New Dangerous Class*, (London and New York: Bloomsbury Academic).

An earlier version of this paper was published in *Dance Research Journal* 49/2 (August 2017).

Energy, Eukinetics, and Effort
Rudolf Laban's Vision of Work and Dance

Susanne Franco

This essay presents Rudolf Laban's understanding of movement and dance as an example of how there cannot be a history of modern dance without both a cultural history of energy as a social construction, as well as a cultural history of work. Dance, like science, participates in a large web of ethical, social and political entanglements, while also constructing models of the moving body. Only by taking account of the reciprocal influences of scientific theories and artists' discourses and practices can we write a history of bodily movement, both onstage and in everyday life.

When Rudolf Laban (1879-1958) started teaching in Germany in the early 1920s, his courses included the study of gesture; the relationship between physical actions, dynamics, and spatial patterns; and the observation of movement and its notation. The issues of movement, space, time, and rhythm were at the core of discourses and practices of dance, but also fundamental to media and technology, as well as psychology, physiology, biology, the European science of work and American time-and-motion studies. Laban studied many of these scientific theories, particularly those concerning the notion of rhythm, which Katya Rothe defines as the »ubiquitous synonym for the new era« (Rothe 2012: 32). Laban considered rhythm to be the ideal tool for connecting people and communities to cosmic laws, and for activating the remembrance of ancient or ›primitive‹ gestures, which were stored in the most archaic layers of our involuntary (collective and personal) memory. In other words, he conceived the body as a crossroads of different kinds of rhythms related to the universe, which itself was also seen as a network of invisible forces. Dance was an instrument for experiencing the world and for displaying the unity of all organic and inorganic matter as an expression of ›harmony‹. Rather than a language of emotionality, Laban considered dance to be a language of action, in which »the various intentions and bodily mental efforts of man are arranged into coherent order« (Laban 1948: 43). The quality of a movement did not depend on the dancer's ability to deal with a complex system of steps and postures, but rather on his/her own attitude toward certain parameters, such as weight, space, time and energy. The vocation of the dancer was to learn to perceive and interpret this energy hidden in the configurations of matter.

Laban built his complex theory of dance by highlighting hidden energies through ecstatic improvisation, as well as by analyzing different parameters of bodily movement by way of a research work that lasted for several decades. Even his notation system reveals modern anthropology's typical ambivalence between the classification of human movements based on scientific and positivistic models, versus a corporeal topology that considered the body to be the materialization of »an eternal cosmic«.

More recently, scholars have considered to what extent Laban's complex theory on movement functioned as a way of introducing and developing new social and political projects, in which the moving body resonated with the vibrations of both the universe and the modern world (Keilson 2013). Laban envisioned a new dimension for dance as a highly elevated form of consciousness in respect to our everyday life, where mystical Freemasonry met the science of work, Nietzsche's philosophy met *Völkisch* ideas, and Romantic anti-capitalism met industrial production. For Laban, the corporeity of modern man was a palimpsest in which to find the traces of a presumed ›original‹ and ›authentic‹ condition, while simultaneously following evolutionist and esoteric theories. He believed that an adaptation to modern life entailed the risk of obliterating memory, alongside the related impoverishment of sensorial and emotional life, as well as limitation of one's ability to relate with the world. The dancer's first task was to develop new skills for connecting him/herself to the rhythmic flows of modern life, and movement became the privileged tool for building a new technology of perception (Baxmann 2000). A dancer trained by Laban was invited to explore, by means of physical actions, his/her own emotional and psychological world and to awaken what he/she imagined as his/her ancestral memory, as well as to move through the space surrounding his/her own body with a deep consciousness of its features and laws. This part of Laban's research drew on the development of 19th century experimental psychology, which was based on evolutionary theories. From this perspective, so called ›tribal societies‹ were characterized by intuition, dynamics, mysticism, and irrationality, and were therefore believed to represent the infancy of humanity and a foundational layer of modern man. The recovery of this archaic intuitive and irrational potential was a *leitmotiv* of German modern dance, which sought to overcome the impoverishment of sensory and emotional experience, and considered the moving body to be the ideal tool for re-immersing the individual in the cosmic continuum.

To investigate the »kinesphere«, as he called the imaginary space around the body, Laban used a set of geometric structures, such as the cube, the octahedron and especially the icosahedron: a volume with twenty faces and twelve spatial directions. A dancer could explore the space inside the icosahedron by practicing different sequences of movements to regain a »natural rhythm« (Laban 1920: 59). Not unlike the crystal that had become the symbol of the *Naturphilosophie*,[1] the icosahedron functioned in Laban's theory as a metaphor of the renewed harmony between nature and dance, as well as a tool for the re-integration of the human being into the cosmos (Laban 1920: 27, 31; Baxmann 2000: 151-160; Guilbert 2000: 33-35). In other words, the way the dancing body creates these tensions and follows the directions of the space corresponds to the organization of nature and therefore, for Laban, »the laws of dance are the law of life« (Laban 1920: 59).

For the philosopher and psychologist Karl Ludwig Klages (who invented graphology, a discipline that measured the vital level of energy invested by an individual in his/her writing), the rhythmic soul was deeply linked to the unconscious memory accessible via dreams, ecstasy and the trance (Klages 1910). Klages, whose thinking profoundly influenced Laban, affirmed that rhythm was the vital principle *par excellence*, which manifested itself in the polarized tensions resulting from an alternation of antagonistic and complementary forces, through which phenomena are renewed and perpetuated. Laban was convinced that the rhythmic movement of the body (*Schwung*) was the perfect tool for activating an immediate form of communication, as well as for giving dancers access to a shared choreography or mass movement through vibrations. Rhythmic movements made mental or psychological states of being visible.

Laban's approach to improvisation was based on the erasure of acquired knowledge to recover the most remote and profound memory for artistic

---

1 The concept of *Naturphilosophie* was introduced by German zoologist Ernst Haeckel (Haeckel 1904).

purposes, followed by the incorporation of new automatisms. He believed that a dancer could develop a condition of »absence-presence« in which to acquire a new ability to perceive hidden energies inside matter, merely using improvisation and the exploration of space. Simultaneously, the study of movement was aimed at enhancing communication skills, developing creativity and kinaesthetic senses, and last but not least, transforming each dancer into a member of a group. Like many other German modern dancers, Laban was also convinced that the rhythmic degeneration of modernity involved the loss of collective rituals, which were capable of establishing a link between the real and the spiritual; the profane and the sacred. Ultimately, this would cause the disappearance of a communitarian dimension, and Laban created his movement choirs as new forms of folk and social dance in the Western world to compensate for the degrading of society in industrial times.

In the 1920s, Laban developed what he called »Choreutics« or »harmony of space«: a branch of his theory that analyzes all possible trajectories of movement into space (directions, levels, plans) by referring to the kinesphere or »the practical study of various forms of (more or less) harmonised movement« (Laban 1966: vii). The book *Choreutics* was published posthumously in 1966, but was written in 1939 to summarize a theory he had been developing since 1913. His approach to »space harmony« was not supported by the desire to create a new aesthetic; his aim was rather to rediscover what he assumed to be the body's natural experience in space and »the *real* structure of human movement and motion in *nature*« (Laban 1966: 5-8). For Laban, space, time and weight were qualities of movement, and he considered them to be forms of acquired knowledge, whereas flow was seen as the dynamic content of movement. By practicing various forms of harmonized movement, he became convinced that human beings might learn to reconnect with nature and their own kinaesthetic dimension, or their state of being.

The exploration of the harmonic laws tied to kinaesthetic energy brought Laban to the development of »Eukinetics«: a branch of Choreutics that determines the dynamic structure of movement (Laban 1966: 30). Eukinetics consists in the analysis of the dynamics and rhythm of movement in time and space, and explores movement trajectories in relations to the origin of movement (central or peripheric), of time (fast or slow), and of energy (strong or light). Later he also defined Eukinetics as the theory of expression and as »a good movement in terms of the harmonious rules of dance« (Laban 1928: 19).

»Effort theory«, which became the focus of Laban's interest in the 1940s in Great Britain, was a direct consequence of these investigations. Whereas Eukinetics applies to the study of what makes a movement »good« in terms of harmonic laws of dance and its expressive qualities, Effort relates to the expressive qualities of the action, which are visible in the rhythm of body movement, and its observation and practice can have a descriptive as well as a prescriptive purpose. Laban's Effort theory is based on the analysis of four motion factors (space, weight, time, and flow), each of which are seen as a continuum between the polarities that constitute the elements or qualities of Effort (direct or indirect, heavy or light, quick or sustained, bound or free). The combination of space, weight, and time produces eight efforts (wring, press, flick, dab, glide, float, punch, slash) that classify styles of movement, as well as speaking to the personality of the person making them. Effort can also be described as the dynamics and qualitative use of energy, or the result of the interplay between the emotional and cognitive attitudes related to movement factors, as well as of the different levels of awareness of each person. More specifically, space is associated with attention and thought, weight with intention and sensation, time with decision and intuition, and flow with progression and feelings. Together they contribute to the phrasing or rhythm of Effort. Despite the fact that there is usually more concern about its expressive aspects, Effort is also functional, and Laban crucially connected the sense of self to physical categories (Flow and Weight), as well as to the environment (Space) over time (Time).

Energetic Bodies, Productive Industries

Until the mid-19th century the fundamental concepts of physics were space, time, mass and a single universal energy that could neither be created or destroyed (*Kraft*). As a hidden and invisible substance embedded in the many natural forms (mechanical, electrical, chemical, and so on), *Kraft* was considered to be capable of advancing society (Rabinbach 1990: 45-68; Campbell 1989: 73-106). Only after the discovery of the second law of thermodynamics was the optimism of energy conservation mitigated by the recognition of its inevitable dissipation and exhaustion. During the industrial revolution in Europe, the metaphor of the »human motor«, introduced in the late 19th century, suggested that the working body was a productive force capable both of transforming universal natural energy into mechanical work, and of linking human organisms to the industrial world. The concept of »labor power« mediated a vision of society powered by a universal energy, wherein the working body represented »one exemplar of that universal process by which energy was converted into mechanical work« (Rabinbach 1990: 1). As Rabinbach summarizes, the metaphor of the »human motor« – a body whose experience was equated with that of a machine – »translated revolutionary scientific discoveries about physical nature into a new vision of social modernity« (Rabinbach 1990: 1). The power of industrial machines and the human (moving and working) body were both measurable because they followed the same dynamic laws: time, space, movement and rhythm.

In Germany, materialism rejected the distinction between the laws of inorganic and organic nature: the cosmos was subsumed under the laws of energy, society was subsumed under the natural law of development, and industrial productivity was only one of its many aspects. In adopting the industrial machine as the new model of the universe, it became the source of energy for industrialized societies. The body and the cosmos became linked by a single flow of energy, and the human motor was at the service of nature: an immense reservoir of energy and power.

In Europe and in the United States, scientists constructed different models of work and of the working body as a performance. They introduced the vision of an economy of energy, the opposite of which was the pathology of work: fatigue. Once the ›ontology‹ of *Kraft* – or the energy able to convert itself into innumerable forms while remaining constant and unchanged – was brought into question by the new concept of entropy and the irreversible decline of energy, fatigue appeared to be *the* last obstacle for progress in modern times (Rabinbach 1990: 39). On the one hand, theories introduced in the United States by Frederic W. Taylor and Frank and Lillian Gilbreth, which included time-and-motion studies for industrial mass production, would improve efficiency and increase productivity by eliminating unnecessary steps and actions. On the other hand, precisely because it was the most evident sign of the external limits of the body (and mind), fatigue became an important parameter for measuring the waste of energy, which in turn was the body's unique capital or its »labor power« (Rabinbach 1990: 7, 19-44). In Europe (and in Russia) physiologists, hygienists, psychologists and, last but not least, dancers and choreographers, all conducted laboratory investigations or invented new techniques for measuring body movement, energy and fatigue.

Both the European science of work and Taylorism were modernist in their promise to liberate industry from the constraints of a society still attached to traditional social attitudes, as well as in predicating the rationalization of the body to augment productivity. However, they differed in their conceptions of the preservation of energy: the European science of work was interested in optimizing it for the sake of society, whereas Taylorism was oriented towards the improvement of industry enterprises. From a European perspective, Taylor's system, which prioritized profit first and foremost, was alarming precisely due to its disregard of both social reforms and the preservation of the workers' body.

The context in which Laban developed his vision of dance and his attention to bodily movement was defined by the convergence of economy, Psychotechnics, Taylorism, and German body culture (Baxmann 2000: 99-118; Baxmann 2009). He was particularly inspired by the German economist Karl Bücher, the author of *Arbeit und Rhythmus* (Labor and Rhythm): a bestseller published in six editions between 1896 and 1924 (Bücher 1896). According to Bücher, »to work is to dance« (Bücher 1896: 334) because rhythm is essentially a bodily element, and its role consists in regulating labor movements favoring the preservation of physical and psychic energies. In order to increase productivity, Bücher suggested restoring natural bodily rhythms and automating movements, because it was only by making them independent of mental control that it was possible to reduce a worker's effort. These theories were very important for overcoming the idea that the most tangible difference between the work of civilized man and that of populations defined as ›primitive‹ or ›wild‹ consisted in the automation of movements. Bücher's analysis overturned the terms of the question and the automation of movements, which were previously considered to be an indication of laziness because they required no mental effort. These now acquired a positive connotation because they preserved and respected the body's natural rhythms as well as its fatigue. It was not industrial labor that caused excessive fatigue, but rather its externally imposed arrhythmic character. In the »revival of love for work« Laban saw the goal of a new dance culture, which wanted to recuperate the condition of humanity as described by Bücher, in which work, dance and play were united (Laban 1920: 128). He was also convinced that

»the level of civilization of a people« depended very much »on the respect for work« because work was »the nerve of life« (Laban 1923: 2).

In the wake of these studies, German *Arbeitswissenschaft* (science of work) advocated an economy of energy, which sought to sustain the nation and promote social happiness through the introduction of rest pauses and training programs. Modern life required an adaptability to changing circumstances, as well as the synchronization of the body's rhythms to those of industrialized life through their repetition, incorporation and transformation into new habits. After the First World War, the psychotechnical craze became quite influential in restructuring the labor market. However, the economic crisis of the late 1920s accentuated critical attitudes toward the science of work, and were blamed for creating unemployment. The disillusionment of rationalization became a new trend, and the idea of work became infused with mystical or transcendental meaning: an authoritarian approach that erased the social neutrality of the European science of work and soon faced the rise of Fascism (Rabinbach 1990: 278-284).

Fritz Giese was a leading expert on Psychotechnic, had been a pupil of Wilhelm Wund and Hugo Münsterberg, and later became a supporter of Nazism. He formulated a series of parameters for calculating ideal worker performance, taking account of his psychological profile and linking an organic notion of the self to the ideal of national regeneration (Killen 2005). Giese, who affirmed that rhythm was a technique for self-regulation, a way to understand modern society, and a potential mean of optimizing labor, exerted great influence upon Laban's theories. Using Giese's perspective on the romantic metaphysics of labor, rhythmic movements became a form of practical intuition rather than theoretical knowledge: not only was behaviour visible in rhythm, it was also controllable through rhythm (Giese 1932). Laban envisioned a new society where technology and the metaphysical dimension of the body, work, ritual and dance could complement one another (Laban 1920: 151):

> All daily acts of labor must be formed out of danced movement. Not only their execution, their form and the form-creating activity of working itself must originate from danced feelings, but also the very choice of the necessity to create. (Laban 1920: 146)

Laban recognized that Taylor (whose *Scientific Management* appeared in its first German translation in 1912, a year after its publication in English) had introduced the first systematic approach to workers' movements, based on the idea of rhythmic efficiency and on energetically and temporally optimized industrial labor. He nonetheless explicitly criticized Taylor's approach (Laban manuscript E (L)/64/88: 2). From Laban's perspective, Taylor's time-and-motion study had not fully developed into a complete industrial instrument because he and his successors neglected the study of human movement. On the contrary, this latter study demonstrated the potential of the European science of work (Laban typescript E (L)/65/13: 1). Laban sought to use his own method to improve work performances via the optimization of motion sequences, but without sacrificing an acceptable level of worker satisfaction in the completion of a task. Laban believed that modernity required a radical change in how it viewed productivity, notably by preserving the quality rather than the quantity of the work, and by privileging bodily and psychological individual skills over industrial needs. The aestheticization of work was the fulfilment of Laban's utopian idea of this new beginning, as well as of the recovery of the original unity of labor, play, and art:

> Industry will no longer disappear from our lives. [...] It is concerned with everyday work and the associated organization of life, as well as with celebrations, recreation, and in art, as it is a matter of making the necessary innovations simple and natural, in terms of the danced concept of life. (Laban 1920: 151)

Based on this cultural background, Laban arrived in Great Britain in the late 1930s and spent the rest of his life primarily researching »Effort« within a wide range of applications, including dance, education and industrial work.

Dancing into Industry

In an unpublished document written toward the end of his career, Laban described his role during his years in Monte Verità near Ascona as a »rhythmical manager«, and addressed a new approach to the correct rhythms for various manual activities (Laban E (L)/76/17: 2). In this alternative community people pursued vegetarianism, grew their own food and wove their clothes. Laban applied the concept of harmony to these different forms of manual labor, from gardening to work in the fields; from kitchen tasks to weaving. He designed specific tasks and rhythmic patterns for each worker. Every activity was accompanied by music and dance, and at the end of the day the workers exchanged reports about what they had done. The process of becoming conscious of their own potentials and limits was considered crucial for assuring the quality of life of the entire community.

In 1929 in Vienna, Laban choreographed *Festzug der Gewerbe* (Pageant of the Trades), a four-mile-long parade of 10,000 representatives of the manual crafts and trades. On this occasion he also had the opportunity to enter studios and workshops, and to observe trade peoples' basic movements, which indicated the different rhythms required in various tasks (Laban 1935: 174-187). He also realized to what extent rhythmic movement directly regulated motivation, and thus productivity, and he became convinced that each worker needed to train his/her individual desires to move and be employed in accordance with his/her own skills.

Laban's experiences in Great Britain's industrial world led him away from his earlier ideals. Although he retrospectively tried to motivate his interest in work and its rhythms by identifying its coherent history since the 1910s, it is evident that the practical necessity of addressing the identity of the German citizen, combined with his professional unemployment during and immediately after the war, primarily pushed him to explore this dimension.

Laban's research became more and more theoretical in the 1940s and 1950s, and this transition is not unrelated to the end of his artistic career. During this time, he developed his research on Eukinetics and specifically on *Antrieb* (internal impulse), which became the core of his Effort theory. The initial phase of these theories can be traced in many of his German texts, where expressions, such as »extreme polarization« or »contrasts« meant something very similar to what Laban later transformed into »elements of effort«. The general scheme, written in German in 1926, was called *Elements of Form Theory* (Laban 1926: 3-5), and probably represents his first attempt to classify movement and the initial synthesis of all of movement's components implied in his notation system, later published in 1928 (Maletic 1987: 54).

This was precisely the notation system that Fredrick Charles Lawrence appreciated about Laban's theory on movement. Lawrence was an engineer and one of the first industrial consultants in Great Britain, whose factories, the Pathon Lawrence & Co. were based in Manchester. He met Laban and his assistant and partner Lisa Ullmann through their common friends, Dorothy and Leonard Elmhirst, who welcomed them in 1938 when they first arrived at Dartington Hall, in the Devonshire countryside of South Western England. In the community of Dartington Laban was able to integrate his visions of dance and movement in other progressive education projects, including communal living and rural reconstruction (Preston-Dunlop 1998: 218-238; Knortz 2008: 117-132). Lawrence was a consultant for the administration of Dartington Rural Industries when he first met Laban, who spent time observing the workers' movements and made his expertise in movement analysis available to improve their performances.

In the early 1940s, Great Britain was fully engaged in the war effort, and the entire population was asked to increase production. The absence of men, many of whom were at the front, had forced factories to employ women and young boys. However, these populations were often physically unsuitable for the roles they had to assume on the assembly line, particularly those in heavy manufacturing. While in the immediate post-war period an urgent need to increase production and to re-employ young people had to be addressed, in the 1950s the government was mainly interested in developing workers' skills, and in adapting production processes to new market needs (Seymour 1954: 3-4; Seymour 1966). When the war was declared, Laban could be classified as a »German alien« by the British Government, and therefore needed to find a way to avoid the (admittedly remote) possibility of ending up in an internment camp. Being involved in the war effort would spare him from this potential outcome. For many reasons, Laban was therefore the right person in the right place and time, and Lawrence understood the great potential of both his approach to movement analysis as well as his notation system, to the degree that they began applying it to industrial work and named it »Industrial Kinetography« (Laban manuscript E (L)/71/9). Unlike other methods based on time-and-motion studies, Laban and Lawrence sought to relieve a worker's effort by analyzing and recording industrial processes, and by examining both rhythmical movements and workers' inner motivations. In 1942 a course called *Rhythmic Movement in Industry* held by Laban and Ullmann was given for a few weeks at Dartington. The exercises designed there to help people work more comfortably and more efficiently later became known as the core of their joint publication *Laban/Lawrence Industrial Rhythm and Lilt in Labour* (Laban-Lawrence 1942). Lawrence, who was able to translate Laban's mystical and philosophical beliefs on movement into management terms, convinced him to move to Manchester where they founded the Management

Training Institute, and Laban was appointed as an adviser at Paton Lawrence & Co. They began developing the potential application of some Eukinetics principles to work on the assembly line, as well as the Personal Effort Assessment: a test that managers could use to evaluate employee's inner motivation. They discarded an early hypothesis of translating the term *Schwung* into *swing*, as it was too connected to the lexicon of popular music. Earlier in Germany, Laban had stated that the future of modern dance belonged to the ›white race‹ because he considered jazz and swing inferior art forms (Laban 1920: 200). They therefore chose the translated term ›Lilt‹, and named their method *Lilt in Labour* or *L.L. Industrial Rhythm*. This consisted of a series of exercises designed to develop the physical strength of new workers, but also sought to sustain their personality and their rhythmic approach to life. They also wanted to increase the efficiency of each company. *The Tyresoles Laban/Lawrence Training Manual* (Laban-Lawrence 1942 T/AD/3/D) was the first booklet specifically addressed to a group of women trained under Laban's supervision.

A volume published in 1947 by Laban and Lawrence was titled *Effort*, and offers the first theoretical and practical guide to training body movement in a working context. In the co-authored book, Laban acknowledged Lawrence for his theoretical collaboration and for the job opportunity he had provided to him. It is interesting to notice that Laban did not do the same for Lisa Ullmann, despite her crucial role and their enduring collaboration.

Laban was convinced that, despite its critical importance, the »rhythmical revival« as a social issue had not received enough attention in modern times. He also believed that the process of civilization caused the loss of a mastery over movement, as well as the degradation of the role of rhythm in labor throughout widespread ›primitive populations‹ (Laban typescript E (L)/65/11: 15). For Laban, dance was the best tool for helping the worker liberate his/her body, and he compared a negative rhythmical pattern in industrial work to the wrong crystalizing processes, during which »bad influences from outside the scope of the formative flow« compromise the potential perfection of its shape (Laban manuscript E (L)/76/11: 6). As Laban and Lawrence affirmed in the introduction of *Effort*:

> Today all that remains of this former rhythmic vitality has been directed into mechanical devices in which the living, driving force of man has been neglected and left without articulate expression. (Laban-Lawrence 1947: 6)

Laban and Lawrence assumed that the control of effort in industry had become an urgent necessity, and they experimented with how it could be discerned in various working actions. To remedy the problem of industrial management in wartime, it was necessary to simplify working procedures, as well as to divide a task previously assigned to a single person amongst several workers. In both cases, an evident reduction of productivity was the result. A good alternative was to enable the worker to quickly perform a task using a series of targeted preparatory exercises. These included a better connection of the required movements, each of which would be executed along with its own counter-movement, and with careful consideration paid to each level of speed and energy (Seymour 1954: 26). For instance, most of the movements completed for industrial work concerned the upper part of the body, so dance could offer the possibility of balancing these through the introduction of a series of compensatory exercises and oscillating movements. Laban and Lawrence compared this compensation with what happened to Western dance when it acquired new kinds of movement from other traditions (Laban typescript E (L)/64/57: 3). The training method they developed for several industries therefore consisted in new movement sequences, designed to relieve fatigue and to »bring that swing and lilt in labor which makes efficiency a pleasure« (Laban-Lawrence 1942 T/AD/3/D: 3). Laban and Lawrence believed that every person invests in weight, time, space and flow in different ways, in order to create a sequence of movements whose intentions are related to a physic or psychic condition. In other words, Effort enables a link between the original inner motivation for the need to move (a sensation, a feeling, a task) and the actual physical movement. For Laban, there was never a single way to perform a task or a movement, and therefore the same worker could perform the same action by following different movement sequences. Laban and Lawrence wanted to highlight the positive and negative aspects of each movement sequence performed by the worker, as well as to particularly identify where the flow was being interrupted (Laban-Lawrence 1942). They consequently analyzed the dynamic and rhythmic qualities of each worker, in order to identify their kinaesthetic and psychological profile for the task to be performed. The results were notated in a simplified version of Laban's notation, called L. L. Industrial Notation (Laban-Lawrence 1947).

The success of the application of the movement sequences suggested by Laban and Lawrence was particularly demonstrated when workers, undertaking long work sessions, experienced reduced fatigue thanks to the cancellation of ›unnecessary movements‹. For each company who used their method, Laban and Lawrence established: a customized ›right way‹ to carry out every single movement; the ›exact duration‹ of a sequence, which always included a moment to rest; and the ›exact amount of energy‹ required to dedicate to the work and its rhythm. In order to improve sales, Laban and Lawrence changed the name of their method to »Personal Effort Assessment«, and then later to the »Laban Lawrence Test«. They also applied it, in movement terms, in order to select and screen candidates for managerial positions. Factories that successfully applied the method included Mars Confectionery, Hoover Ltd., and even the UK Air Ministry. Following an interview that Laban gave in the mid 1950s, the factories in which his method was applied increased their productivity by up to 50 %, although no documented proof was provided for this affirmation (Moore 1954: 60). No trace of independent analysis verifying the results of these assessments and programs exist, and yet what seems to have diminished during this time was Laban's original assertion that there was no single way to perform a task at work. On the contrary, Laban and Lawrence progressively ›cleaned‹ movements, and standardized what they assumed to be the ›correct‹ motor sequences, primarily for the sake of industrial production. In the end, the logic of quantity prevailed over quality, and industrial tasks took precedence over individual skills.

At the same time, Laban had to maintain all possibilities for the development and use of his Effort theory without precluding the artistic field. He insisted that people *do* in fact use the same efforts in all the activities he had specified as including expressive gestures. He frequently repeated not only that dance should enter the industrial world, but also that the *L. L. Industrial Rhythm* could reveal its potential for connecting dance to »the reality of our present life« (Laban typescript E(L)/31/39: 2):

> The incorporation of artistic elements is unavoidable as soon as one makes use of rhythm. This is the reason why it is justified to speak of introduction to ›Art of Movement into Industry‹ and this interrelation of art and science in the future will be considered as one of the outstanding features of a progressing industrial civilization. (Laban E (L)/65/70: 13)

Laban and Lawrence described the »Art of Industry« or the »Dance into Industry« as »a living reality with enormous possibilities« (Laban typescript E(L)/65/11: 13) and they ultimately compared a worker to a dancer:

A dancer does not use his arms, his legs and his mind more than a tramway conductor or a worker dealing with a press, because every human being uses movement and therefore the study of movement is vital if we aim at leading each person's energy to the best possible use for his/her satisfaction or to execute in the best way the task his/her need to execute. (Laban typescript E(L)/33/51: 1)

Lawrence believed that rhythm was the most cohesive of all motion factors, and that the right proportion between all rhythmic elements in a motion sequence introduced an unusual but important element: beauty (Lawrence 1943: 131). »Industry« as he affirmed »requires movements that comprise the whole scale of dance and recreation, and can with profit turn to them to learn, at long last, how to move easily, well and to good effect« (Laban typescript E (L)/65/13: 2). Laban also introduced the vision of a »symphony of production« (Laban-Lawrence 1942: 15):

When entering a well running factory, the first thing that strikes you is the rhythm of the work. The rhythm of all activities evolving before your eyes and impressing our ears can easily be compared with the rhythm of movements and sounds in an orchestra. (Laban typescript E(L)/76/2: 11)

Laban's Effort theory introduced in Great Britain a way of thinking about energetic forces as forms of aesthetic intervention. This was not unlike what had been widely experienced during the 1920s in Russia at the Moscow Central'nyj Institute Truda (Central Institute of Work). Laban was aware of this context, wherein a team of scholars and artists focused on the well-being of the workers, and sought to make their movements more attractive. This was intended to create new art forms and performances in order to disseminate new approaches to Taylorism (Misler 2017: 161-180).

A Poem of Effort

After the end of the war, Laban adapted his approach to Effort to different contexts and presented it in different books. *Modern Educational Dance* (1948), reprinted five times, was the most widely read and probably the most influential of his writings. *The Mastery of Movement on the Stage* (1950, and the following editions) reworked Effort theory to apply it to dance as well as to mime and acting. Other texts, such as *The Introduction of the Art of Movement into Industry* (Laban typescript E(L)/65/70), *Dancing into Industry* (Laban typescript E(L)/33/51), and *Road Connecting Dance and Industry* (Laban manuscript E(L)/65/12) remained unpublished. Contained within these archival material is a project for a film on Effort – unfortunately, like most of the others, not realized – that bears witness to what extent Laban believed in the potential of his theory (Laban manuscript L/E/42/27; Franco 2012).

What is known today as Laban Movement Analysis and Effort theory is a theoretical and experiential system for the observation, description, prescription, performance, and interpretation of human movement, and provides an understanding for developing both expressiveness and efficiency. Laban's German cultural background is rarely recognized by most practitioners, particularly in the British (dance) educational system, in which it has long since been extensively integrated. The ideologically complex and controversial substance of Laban's theory (Kant 2002; Vertinsky 2007) also seems to have been forgotten amidst the growing field that is defined under the umbrella term »somatics«, where today many aspects of Laban's theory are indirectly transmitted. In this context, Effort theory has contributed to the idea that not only are weight, affect and psychology intertwined with each other, and able to describe our way of being in the world, but also that they represent tools for a deep transformation of a dancer's body and imagination. In other words, matter seems to be the only path to a person's most profound transformation, and Effort theory investigates the deepest input that causes movement and enables its transformation.

Laban introduced the idea that dance is a »poem of effort« through which we can constantly reinvent our own physical matter and make our bodily, mental and emotional energies circulate (Laban 1959: 37). A cultural history of dance should make these concepts and their complex ideological origins circulate as well.

Works Cited

Baxmann, Inge (2009): »Arbeit und Rhythmus. Die Moderne und der Traum von der glücklichen Arbeit.« In: M. Gruß/S. Göschel/V. Lauf (eds.): *Arbeit und Rhythmus. Lebensformen im Wandel*, (Paderborn: Wilhelm Fink Verlag), pp. 15-36.

Baxmann, Inge (2000): *Mythos Gemeinschaft. Körper- und Tanzkulturen in der Moderne*, (München: Wilhelm Fink Verlag).

Bücher, Karl (1896): *Arbeit und Rhythmus*, (Leipzig: Abhandlungen der Königl. Sächsischen Gesellschaft der Wissenschaften).

Campbell, Joan (1989): *Joy in Work, German Work. The National Debate, 1800-1945*, (Princeton: Princeton University Press).

Davies, Eden (2006): *Beyond Dance. Laban's Legacy of Movement Analysis*, (London and New York: Routledge).

Franco, Susanne (2012): *Rudolf Laban's Dance Film Projects*. In: Susan Manning/Lucia Ruprecht (eds.): *German Dance Studies*, (Urbana-Chicago-Springfield: University of Illinois Press), pp. 63-78.

Giese, Fritz (1925): *Theorie der Psychotechnik*, (Braunschweig: Vieweg).

Giese, Fritz (1932): *Philosophie der Arbeit*, (Halle: Marhold).

Guilbert, Laure (2012 [2000]): *Danser avec le IIIe Reich. Les danseurs modernes sous le nazisme*, (Bruxelles: Complexe).

Haeckel, Ernst (1904): *Kunstformen der Natur*, (Leipzig-Vienna: Verlag des Bibliographischen Institut).

Kant, Marion (2002): »Laban's Secret Religion«, *Discourses in Dance*, 2/1, pp. 43-62.

Keilson, Ana Isabel (2013): *Making Dance Knowledge: Politics and Modern Dance in Germany, 1890 – 1927*, (PhD in History, Columbia University).

Killen, Andreas (2005): *Berlin Electropolis. Shock, Nerves, and German Modernity*, (Oakland: University of California Press).

Klages, Ludwig (1910): *Die Probleme der Graphologie. Entwurf einer Psychodiagnostik*, (Leipzig: Verlag von Johann Ambrosius Barth).

Knortz, Heike (2008): »Vom Tanz zum ›industrial rhythm‹. Rudolph von Labans System der Bewegungsanalyse.« In: Reinhold Bauer, James Williams, Wolfhard Weber (eds.): *Technik zwischen artes und arts: Festschrift für Hans-Joachim Braun*, (Münster, Waxmann), pp. 117-132.

Laban, Rudolf (1920): *Die Welt des Tänzers. Fünf Gedankenreigen*, (Stuttgart: Seifert).

Laban, Rudolf (1923): *Was ist Arbeit?*, manuscript, pp. 1-11, Nachlass Rudolf von Laban, Mappe IV: Rep. 028 IV. b1 (N°59), (Tanzarchiv Leipzig).

Laban, Rudolf (1926): *Choreographie*, (Jena: Diederichs).

Laban, Rudolf (1928): *Schrifttanz- Methodik, Orthographie, Erläuterungen*, (Wien and Leipzig: Universal Edition).

Laban, Rudolf (1935): *Ein Leben für den Tanz. Erinnerungen*, (Dresden: Carl Riessner Verlag).

Laban, Rudolf (1943): *Early Notes on Industry. Dancing as a Recreative Activity*, typescript, 30-3-1943, pp. 1-5, E(L)/64/57, (The Laban Archives, National Resource Centre for Dance, University of Surrey).

Laban, Rudolf (1945): *Historical Notes about the Development of Movement and Working Rhythms* (part of an unpublished book project), manuscript, 29-11-1945, E(L)/64/88, (The Laban Archives, National Resource Centre for Dance, University of Surrey).

Laban, Rudolf (1947): *The Introduction of the Art of Movement into Industry*, typescript, 5-12-1947, E(L)/65/70, pp. 1-13, (The Laban Archives, National Resource Centre for Dance, University of Surrey).

Laban, Rudolf (1948): *Modern Educational Dance*, (London: Macdonald & Evans).

Laban, Rudolf (1951): *Dancing into Industry. A Non Technical Explanation of Technique Now in Use in Industry for The Selection and Training of Operatives and Junior Managers. Movement Notation and Interpretation*, typescript, pp. 1-4, E(L)/33/51, (The Laban Archives, National Resource Centre for Dance, University of Surrey).

Laban, Rudolf (1959): »Dance as a Discipline«, *L.A.M.G. Magazine*, 22, p. 37.

Laban, Rudolf (1966 [1939]): *Choreutics*, annotated and edited by Lisa Ullmann (London: MacDonald & Evans).

Laban, Rudolf (1975): *A Life for Dance. Reminiscences*, (London: MacDonald & Evans).

Laban, Rudolf (n. d.): *Industrial Rhythm in Dance Education*. Conference by Laban at the Contemporary Dance Club London, typescript, E(L)/31/39, pp. 1-6, (The Laban Archives, National Resource Centre for Dance, University of Surrey).

Laban, Rudolf (n. d.): *Lecture for the Birmingham and London Contemporary Dance Clubs*, typescript, p. 11, E(L)/76/2, (The Laban Archives, National Resource Centre for Dance, University of Surrey).

Laban, Rudolf (n.d.): *Dance in Present Day Society. Chapter 1* (probably part of an unpublished book project), typescript, pp. 12-22, E(L)/65/11, (The Laban Archives, National Resource Centre for Dance, University of Surrey).

Laban, Rudolf (n.d.): *Dartington Hall 1942. Industrial Kinetography*, manuscript, pp. 1-7, E(L)/71/9, (The Laban Archives, National Resource Centre for Dance, University of Surrey).

Laban, Rudolf (n.d.): *First Experiments with Industrial Rhythm*, manuscript, E(L)/76/17, (The Laban Archives, National Resource Centre for Dance, University of Surrey).

Laban, Rudolf (n.d.): *Industrial Rhythm*, manuscript, pp. 1-16, E(L)/76/11, (The Laban Archive, National Resource Centre for Dance, University of Surrey).

Laban, Rudolf (n.d.): *Notes on a film on Effort, Erinnerungen*, pp. 1-4, L/E/42/27, (The Laban Archives, National Resource Centre for Dance, University of Surrey).

Laban, Rudolf (n.d.): *Road Connecting Dance and Industry* (chapter n. 3 of an unpublished book project), manuscript, pp. 43-46, NRCD, E(L)/65/12, (The Laban Archives, National Resource Centre for Dance, University of Surrey).

Laban, Rudolf (n.d.): *Dance into Industry. Introduction* (probably part of an unpublished book project *Dance into Industry*), typescript, p. 1, E(L)/65/13, (The Laban Archives, National Resource Centre for Dance, University of Surrey).

Laban, Rudolf/Fredrick C. Lawrence (1947): *Effort. Economy of Human Movement*, (London: Macdonald and Evans).

Laban, Rudolf/Fredrick C. Lawrence (1942): *Laban/Lawrence Industrial Rhythm and Lilt in Labour*, (Manchester: Paton & Lawrence & Co.).

Laban Rudolf, Fredrick C. Lawrence (1942): *The Tyresoles Laban/Lawrence Training Manual*, T/AD/3/D/, (The Dartington Hall Trust Archive, Manchester).

Lawrence, Fredrick C. (1943): »The Key to Motion Study«, *Journal of Physical Education and School Hygiene*, November, p. 131.

Maletic, Vera (1987): *Body, Space, Expression: The Development of Rudolf Laban's Movement and Dance Concepts*, (Berlin: Walter de Gruyter).

Misler, Nicoletta (2017): *The Russian Art of Movement*, (Milano: Allemandi).

Moore, Olive (1954): »Man of the Month, Rudolf Laban«, *Scope. Magazine for Industry*, pp. 60-86.

Preston-Dunlop, Valerie (1998): *Rudolf Laban. Extraordinary Life*, (London: Dance Books).

Rabinbach, Anson (1990): *The Human Motor. Energy, Fatigue, and the Origins of Modernity*, (New York: Basic Books).

Rothe, Katya (2012): »Economy of Human Movement. Performances of Economic Knowledge«, *Performance Research*, n. 7, vol. 17 (*On Labour & Performance*), Gabriele Klein, Bojana Kunst (eds.), pp. 32-39.

Seymour, W. D. (1954): *Industrial Training for Manual Operations*, (London: Pitman & Sons).

Seymour, W. D. (1966): *Industrial Skills*, (London: Pitman & Sons).

Vertinsky, Patricia (2007): »Movement Practices and Fascist Infections: From Dance Under the Swastika to Movement Education in the British Primary School«. In: Jennifer Hargreaves, Patricia Vertinsky (eds.), *Physical Culture, Power and the Body*, (New York and London: Routledge), pp. 25-51.

Artistic Perspectives on
Somatic Interventions

Margrét Sara Guðjónsdóttir's »Full Drop into the Body«
A Conversation with Susan Kozel and a Public Discussion

SUSAN KOZEL: One of the striking things about Margrét Sara's work is that she does not just use somatic practices to train the body before setting a choreography upon it. What Margrét Sara does is work with somatic practices as a meditative myofascial release to create bodily states. Those states are then choreographed. Reflecting on this unique approach to bodily practice as choreography, a two-fold question arises: firstly, can you explain your specific practice, called »Full Drop into the Body«? And secondly, can you describe how this leads into choreography?

MARGRÉT SARA GUÐJÓNSDÓTTIR: In 2010 I began to research a certain bone visualization meditation, which induces a deep myofascial release. My first encounter with this visualization meditation occurred while I was working for another performance maker, together with my friend the German dancer and fascia therapist Anja Röttgerkamp. When I had confessed to her that I was tired after rehearsal, she replied: »Just lie down on the floor and melt your bones. It will ground you and when you stand up again you are going to be full of energy, I use it as a warm up before performing.« However, what happened to me was very different. I laid down on the floor, performed the meditation, and discovered I could not stand up again. Instead I came deeply into touch with the incredible exhaustion of my matter and spirit, which in turn totally changed my life and interest in body and dance work.

I therefore spent the next three years on the floor practicing this meditation, up to five hours a day, and experiencing all kinds of full-body states, rhythms of inner systems, and inner movements. In relation to this, I noticed a strong wish to cease performing and to de-condition my hyper-professional dancer's body. I came into dialogue with my tissue regarding exhaustion and a resistance to performing in this achievement-oriented society, which had caused me use the force of my muscles and the force of my will to get what I thought I wanted to achieve. Although my career as a dancer and maker has been conducted within the experimental field of contemporary dance, I trained as a gymnast as a child. You can imagine how much conditioning had become normal to me since that time: to push through and over all my limits, in order to achieve and succeed on all levels. I began this meditation eight years ago and it has been my practice ever since.

Of course, it has also developed tremendously over these past eight years. I discovered new tools to enter ever more deeply into dialogue and intimacy, both with myself via the body, as well as with and through the dancers I work with. Getting in touch with the tissues of a burnt-out body – an alienated, isolated, disconnected and non-sensing body – directly reflects the sociopolitical situation we live in. This is a society of speed and isolation, where identity and self-value are built on personal achievements and competition, not unlike in professional sports. We are all in this space, and it expresses itself and is reflected in the matter of which we are made. In response, I started to develop a practice of utter surrender. Of not doing anything. Of letting go of control and basically not moving until something else did: something more than my will and my conditioned body moving habitually through muscular force or my dancer's body memory. Out of this practice I discovered multiple inner rhythms. Once you stop *doing* and start *listening*, you develop a whole new relationship with yourself, because you have developed a sort of neutral observant eye upon yourself that can, through its neutrality, guide you into sensing and being with yourself in much subtler, deeper ways, and in non-dualistic terms. Another reality of yourself opens up to you. I researched the tides and the rhythms of the tides, some of which cranio-sacral therapists also work with. I got in touch with that inner breath that is the biorhythm: a certain type of autonomous rhythm in the body that never stops and has its own timing, as well as a lot of other rhythms that are constantly beating in your body without you feeling or recognizing them in your daily life. So, it is a form of hyper-inner-listening that I started to practice. At a certain point something moved me, and it made my body move without my consciously controlling the movement or knowing where it was taking me. This became a breakthrough into recognizing a certain type of inner movement that can actually animate your body visibly. I began to train myself in how to get in touch, on demand, with these inner movements, and I discovered the modes of different speeds and pathways within the body. When I eventually shared this inner listening and started teaching people how to connect with this inner movement, I noticed the tremendous amount of presence it created. This presence was very touching for me in the way it demands one's attention. I work with it consciously in my performances.

In 2013 I was commissioned to do a graduation performance work for the BA dance students at the DOCH – Uniarts in Stockholm. As I believed it necessary for me to have a common language with the students in order to complete this work, I decided to teach them this practice of inner listening. The piece was titled *Step Right To It* and the process was both beautiful and also represented my own beginning of sharing and developing this kind of practice with others. Previously I had been doing the practice solely by myself, away from the context of performance making, and in order to step out of the exhausted professional dancer's body and to release it from its conditioned body memory. This is how it started entering my choreographic works and how it has developed alongside other artistic themes since.

During the years 2014-2015 I worked on the *Blind Spotting Performance Series*: placing the burnt-out, broken, exhausted, apathetic, imploding body of the achievement-oriented society and the anonymous multitude on display in front of red velvet theatre curtains. My deep and artistic desire for the series was to build a space on the contemporary stage for the antihero, especially in the context of dance. We do not need any more polished controlled, or aesthetic bodies to watch: we have these everywhere around us on billboards. Instead we are talking about resistance and about placing more importance on what things feel like rather than what they look like. It is also about highlighting topics such as vulnerability and overexposure, as well as the need for intimacy and dialogues with inner, physical, psychological and emotional pathologies and realities. Between 2015-2017 I decided to create certain conditions, for myself and the dancers I have worked with before, by conducting a two-year research period into opening up a new branch of my practice, while still keeping focus on the introspective body: moving away from the exhausted, broken and emptied out body, into a more energized, private emotional body. I wanted to work with the expression of the pathological inner symphonies of the private emotional body with which we are all constantly, albeit mostly unconsciously, in dialogue. The dancers and I started to work on how to dive into the subconscious and unconscious, and we reached a new and intense territory together. We used meditation to tune into hidden realities – blind spots, so to speak – in order to allow unknown knowledge and states to appear to us through the matter. As a result, a new work entitled *Conspiracy Ceremony – HYPERSONIC STATES* premiered in November 2017 at the Sophiensaele, here in Berlin.

SUSAN KOZEL: I would like to ask you to speak, from your choreographer's perspective, about your choreographic sensibilities. Once you have worked with dancers who have done this practice for a very long time, and you have identified pathological states, then you need to shape them into a piece that lasts roughly 60 minutes, such as *Conspiracy Ceremony – HYPERSONIC STATES*. Can you describe how you make the transition to the conventions of the professional dance production world while still remaining faithful to the energetic forces of the meditative practice?

MARGRÉT SARA GUÐJÓNSDÓTTIR: As you can imagine, it is quite a job to develop choreographic processes when beginning from the position of dancers lying down on the floor. They are experiencing a lot sensorially, and coming into incredible intimacy with themselves, along with undergoing a kind of widening of the recognition and awareness of themselves through their own matter. However, very little of this wild inner life and experiential field is visible from the outside. The dancers lie on the floor, in ecstatic states at times, and yet I see nothing: no expression and no movement.

For that piece (*Conspiracy Ceremony – HYPERSONIC STATES*) I set out to research an artistic topic that required a certain type of body and movement vocabulary (the *hyperstates*) on stage to convey it. I would then compose these *hyperstates* as if they were notes in a musical score, because each *hyperstate* has its own color and feeling, just like musical notes do. My inspiration for conducting these two years of research was to discover more animated, complex and inter-personally linked states that could arise from not only autonomous inner body systems, but also from the subconscious levels of each individual dancer. They were unique expressions of the non-expressed but highly active component of a person's being. I have called them *hyperstates*, since they are colored by emotional and formerly lived experiences. What I discovered during this long working process was that, eventually, all sorts of physical states arise. This is because an increasingly deep capacity to surrender to what is there develops, along with a perpetually deepening access to your inner depths. As a desired result, this performance became very different from the others, and of course it also brought into other territories such as the archetypes of the common unconscious. These explicitly became the main topic of my newest work premiering at the Sophiensaele in November 2018, titled *Pervasive Magnetic Stimuli.*

Figure 1: *Pervasive Magnetic Stimuli.* Choreographed by Margrét Sara Guðjónsdóttir, Sophiensaele Berlin 2018.

In *Conspiracy Ceremony – HYPERSONIC STATES* we searched endlessly for openings. We asked: how can inner, personal, private, subjective, sensorial experiences and inner realities reveal full body states? How can they be visible from the outside? How can the audience feel it in their own bodies? We work with activated and »volume-ized« connective tissue movements, and if you experience these performing bodies live on stage the connectivity stretching from body to body is palpably present in the theatre between the dancers and audiences. Actually, you can create a direct physical connection with the audience, and they will feel what is happening in front of their eyes but now within their own bodies. This point has always been very important for me: how can I reach this level of »communication« through the performances? How can I make a performance with this kind of oozing energetic body, while at the same time talking about its tragic state? My wish is to reach a kind of mirroring of this togetherness, an opening and a letting happen, so as to give space for these topics of shared realities to emerge through the body. I worked on these *hyperstates* during 2015-2017. It was a process of stepping out of my extremely precise director's position, up to a certain degree, and collectively discovering inner pathways and keys to stage full authentic body states, via very personal and new types of dialoging with the dancers. The dancers could then access these states again and again. The primary goals were to truly live in these states in front of the audience, as well as that the states would create their own animated movements or static positions, each with different types of flavors, timing, colors and autonomous hyper-privateness. Based upon these experiences I have been able to expand the vocabulary of the *Full Drop into the Body* practice, and ultimately created the performance *Conspiracy Ceremony – HYPERSONIC STATES* out of it.

As with each of my works since 2010, I still use my »eagle eye« to spot, distill, and then mold and direct the material in very concrete ways. This allows it to be able to serve its artistic purpose, and for it to be received as fully as possible, as well as to be performed on demand within a detailed and composed performance. I spent the last eight years in this busy pursuit and it is quite important for me to now share this reality with people, and to see what kind of repercussions and cognitive shifts occur as a result of that sharing. My interest lies in finding ways of developing the capacity for cognitive plasticity through activating the fascial body.

Susan Kozel: Can you say something about the broken body, because you speak a lot of pathologies and choreographing through them? And also about the way the dancers' bodies are mirroring what you are seeing in the world?

Margrét Sara Guðjónsdóttir: [directing the question to the audience] What do you think? What do you do with your blockages? Sadness? Incapacities? Your exhaustion?

When dancers follow this inner listening I propose to them, that I can observe through their bodily movements clear expressions of blockages in certain areas, as well as incoherencies in amplitude, rhythm, and the direction of movement of internal and energetic systems. Pathologies. I have developed a keen eye for those bodies as well as the wish for them to be visible, spoken about, choreographed and worked with in the dance sector. My piece *Step Right To It* (2013) was the first performance where I used my practice as a working tool. I wanted to work choreographically with bodies that appeared to have no awareness of being the servants of a larger political power, which wants them to be and behave in a certain way. They are almost like cold, empty, numb bodies participating in actions without thinking. These are the generic young bodies of the digital millennium generation. I was placing emphasis upon total isolation, as well as upon the alienation of those bodies. They were spiritless and disconnected from themselves, from the outside, and from each other. In the *Blind Spotting Performance Series* (2014-2015) I focused on showcasing and working with the exhausted broken matter of the burned out body, which perhaps was more directed at the bodies of people in their thirties and forties. These are the bodies of people who became overwhelmed by neoliberal society's demands on the individual. They are extremely slow, darkly flavored bodies, incapable of reaching out, reacting, moving or being vibrant in any way. Imploding, and over-flowing with too much information, oozing, peeing, drooling, unable to keep things in anymore. Bodies without life energy.

In order to choreograph performances about these topics you require bodies that embody these states, rather than bodies that showcase their dance control. I direct the material by stripping away all referential or habitual movements, directions, and the tonus in the body that does not support these states when they are observed from the outside. This undoing of the physical habits of the dancers I work with requires a lot of work. At all times I need them to look very pedestrian and non-composed, and I place great focus and emphasis upon this, so the crafting of the material and simplifying of a lot of gestures and movements becomes the hidden acrobatic-ism of my work. What appears to be very natural timing is in fact completely composed, in order to create that effect on stage.

Choreographically, I specifically work to offer the audience the most precise, detailed and clear propositions possible. I do so by stripping away everything that does not serve this purpose, to create maximum clarity, in order for the audience to have as much freedom as possible to perceive it. The work therefore does not dominate the mind and its reflections, but rather determines the audience members' physical experiences, which also serve to hold their attention. This occurs if the audience allow themselves to fall into the physical dialogue that is resonating so strongly in the room, due to the physical practice. What the dancers practice, and what I myself strive for as the performance choreographer, is to offer an experience where one can fully surrender to the physical sensorial experience of the event, while at the same time maintaining an extremely clear cognitive clarity and awareness. Contradictions always exist inside each other.

QUESTION FROM THE AUDIENCE: You were talking about tissues and the connectedness or connectivity between people and the dancers. Do you think there is something like this connective tissue between persons, or between a dancer and their movements and the space around them?

MARGRÉT SARA GUÐJÓNSDÓTTIR: I do not separate the dancers from the inner movements and full body states that they dance with and which dance them. And yes, the space where the happening of the performances takes place, between the dancers and the audience, can be filled with connective tissue energy/movement. The physical performance is infiltrating the body of the audience, which happens through the connective tissue. This has been experienced time and again by different audience members and critics who otherwise do not know anything about myofascial work.

SUSAN KOZEL: In my experience and research into Margrét Sara's practice, she uses language very carefully to communicate and to give choreographic guidance to the dancers. She has developed a way of using words to nudge them back into a particular state if they have happened to slip out of it. Indeed, when the dancers slip out of an energetic state, the field collapses; it is just not there anymore. This observation opens a direct link with the different kinds of energetic forces that we are discussing today at this conference. Energetic forces have a clear somatic validity. They are not only visual or sensory, rather these forces invite different ways of using language in choreographic processes. In the case of Margrét Sara's work, this language is fascinating because it ranges from recognizable terms for bodily states and emotions (such as hate, love or ecstasy), but also includes less definable qualities (like black slime, trauma, possession, and hesitation), figures (like snowman, sculpture garden and Jesus-woman), and actions (like flavoring, puffing-up, crushing and becoming). This curious use of language borders on the affective and imaginary. Margrét Sara, can you say more?

MARGRÉT SARA GUÐJÓNSDÓTTIR: I think a very big part of my work is that, with each and every person that I work with, we have to create our own vocabulary of understanding in order to find ways of describing our inner subjective experiences, and that is why it takes so long. By now I have a large knowledge of possible reactions and states that can be experienced by people who do the *Full Drop into the Body* practice. These elements and processes are something that I can teach and guide people towards, but there are also the *hyperstates*, which are the newer branch of the method the dancers and I searched for during the last two years. These are personal individual states and trips, which the dancers experience, and many of them feel amazing and yet at the same time look like nothing. At times you cannot observe the experience in the/of the body from the outside. So it is strenuous work to do, and it takes a very long time to work in this way and especially in order to create a performative outcome. But when you witness someone in front of you actually living something profoundly deep, you recognize the process that it kick-starts in your own being. Then you realize that this is a very strong thing, and that is why I dedicate my time to this kind of work. And now I am of course very trained in how to bring something into focus in the studio, in terms of dialog, state and movement-material.

This work we are actually busy with is not about shape, nor is it about a spectacular movement quality. Rather, this type of full presence and these magical physical qualities that appear through the practice are used choreographically in order to carry a larger message – emphasizing physical communication and the activation of new states, thoughts, consciousness and realities for both the viewers and performers.

These working processes are very private, which has become apparent ever since I started to work with long term collaborators in 2013, and those dancers have a lot of experience with the method by now. When you work like this, you make the decision to go into depths that exceed professionalism. It becomes a private and personal journey that you nonetheless share with the group, no matter what happens. In our long relationship, my collaborators and I have discovered that the work goes together with friendship, and that is very important. Additionally, I have also developed ways to give classes and workshops to professional dancers, as well as to people outside the artistic field. Separating performance-making from the practices, and using my own experiences with the practice to create a safe space for inner listening and myofascial release, creates conditions for people to come into intimacy with themselves and with their tissues, which is the main priority.

QUESTION FROM THE AUDIENCE: I would like to ask if you could say something about the sound in your performance, because I was deeply intrigued by the sound. I had the image in my mind of listening to inner body processes, while watching bodies performing them.

MARGRÉT SARA GUÐJÓNSDÓTTIR: To »color« the performances, I use the experimental and very sensorial music of Peter Rehberg – who is an electronic musician originally from London and now living in Austria directing the record label MEGO. I have worked with Peter since 2010 and when we devise the performances I guide him onto certain paths. Together we make it work, but the music is mostly created and worked upon separately.

QUESTION FROM THE AUDIENCE: And does the music have the function to trigger certain states?

MARGRÉT SARA GUÐJÓNSDÓTTIR: The dancers can reach these states without the music, due to the way we work and train together. It comes from a deep listening to the body. Actually, the music is there for the audience, and I use it consciously to embrace the audience, or to confuse them, or to guide them into a slower rhythm. For me, it is a choreographic question of how to use the music in each piece, and I operate with the music in different ways. Sometimes it is intended to make it harder for the audience to be with the dancers, or sometimes easier. Often it is to add a color and a topic for thought in relations to the visuals, so to speak. Most of the time I work conceptually with the music, but the sound of course has a very sensorial as well as a referential quality.

QUESTION FROM THE AUDIENCE: I would like to ask you again about your use of language, since I am wondering if you address affects in particular and/ or do you verbally create and figure landscapes or images like, for example, flowing water? Summing up, my main question is: do you address affects directly or do you use other imagery to stimulate them? Or do you look for something other than affects?

MARGRÉT SARA GUÐJÓNSDÓTTIR: I use visualizations that trigger the participant fascial system which leads the way to a meditative practice. What you discover through this practice is your own immense sensorial subjective experience field of inner listening. In this way the work differs greatly from practices such as hypnosis, trance, past life transgression, Mysore yogic meditations or other ways of getting in touch with the energies of the subtle body, the subconscious and beyond.

SUSAN KOZEL: I find it fascinating that it was so hard to ask that last question on affect, because what you (the questioner) are navigating is the distinction between somatic states and affects. These overlap and swarm around each other, and as much as we need to ask ourselves to define them and distinguish them, they sort of collapse together again, making the work of understanding them analytically even harder. I have a feeling that Margrét Sara, and each of us who experience her work, might be able to come up with our own senses of where the affect resides in relation to the somatic, and how these are materialized through the processes. But this is a shifting terrain, because affects are, as far as I understand them, exchanges of intensities. They are already there, they are generated, and they exist as potential. Affects exist above and beyond the emotional body: they exist as vibrations.

MARGRÉT SARA GUÐJÓNSDÓTTIR: I just want to say that when you work in the way that I am working, you leave a lot of space for the subjective sensorial experiences that are unique to each person. That is why the mapping of working in this way is particularly exciting and difficult.

QUESTION FROM THE AUDIENCE: I am very, very fascinated. Thank you. I am wondering how much care goes into this; the ethics of it. There is a lot of exposure in this work. My question would be: it seems to be incredibly difficult to navigate a line between these melting bodies crying, and then choreographing them. For a performer it seems to me to be extremely difficult to then re-impose form on this, so that you can re-perform it on stage. Do you see what I mean? It is of course relatively fraught, or very very difficult ethically. I find this very fascinating, but it is probably very hard. How do you do it?

MARGRÉT SARA GUÐJÓNSDÓTTIR: I will explain. When you work with this *Full Drop Practice* it is deeply healing. This is very clear between those of us who work together. We seek to elevate the performers capacity to be in the here and now; to be with the whole of herself. Increasing presence. I create working conditions for ceasing active doing, in order to come into full presence through self-exploration. This becomes a task where there are no boundaries between the private and the professional. That has been clear from day one, and the people with whom I work joined the project due to that same desire. It is a trip, as well as a massive self-exploration and de-conditioning, and a freeing of matter through work on structural adjustments, changes and integration.

The dancers I work with are all professionally very experienced performers, and I would say that what we do is impossible if you are not a professional dancer, since the type of analysis and awareness we are currently working with is quite advanced. This is what enables us to make a performative stage work from it, as well as a personal practice. They go on stage without feeling exposed since the framing and crafting of the performance work protects their autonomy and their privacy. As a viewer you also feel their power in what they do, making it impossible to feel like you are some sort of a »Peeping Tom«. I work consciously and clearly with this topic, and control the outcome in that way: the work is thoroughly composed. And that is, of course, my deepest desire as a choreographer, to make work where you can talk about this over-exposure and intimacy without exploiting anybody in that performance space, being in the rawness of that topic and reality nevertheless. That is a very political issue for me and is deeply important. If you could experience the pieces you would understand better what I am talking about. What you observe is the darkness of the topic being addressed in each piece, but working on it is deeply healing, and even pleasurable. Many of the states in my works perceived from the outside as very dark are actually experienced by the dancers as incredibly enjoyable in their bodies, even if they are drooling and peeing. It is a wonderful thing to heal directly through artistic processes. It is deeply humanistic work.

QUESTION FROM THE AUDIENCE: My question concerns your strong ties to a philosophically phenomenological approach and aesthetic. I am wondering about your scientific sources, or other material you refer to in your body work, especially about your fascia knowledge. To what degree much do you bring the knowledge that we currently have about fascia to your project? I would be curious to know more, because it is probably not a bibliography. So what kind of sources were you looking for to sustain your research?

MARGRÉT SARA GUÐJÓNSDÓTTIR: I will go into this topic more in the workshop immediately after this talk. By now it has been proven that the bones are compressed fascia. Basically, we have a tremendous amount of fascia in our body that is either very compressed or completely liquid: it is all the same. You carry your whole life with you in your tissues. Everything you experience. The fascia does this. Say you fall off your bike or somebody hurts you emotionally: your tissue is reacting to it, leaving tightness, blockages or scars. Mostly, if you do not react to it instantly, you carry it with you in your body from then on, wherever you are. That is usually what people call »old people's bodies«, which are actually just an accumulation of hardened fascia, and people closing their bodies more and more as a naturally protective physical device. When you start to work with this matter, which is focused on initiating movement and unblocking areas that are blocked, you will address the fascia in the body and then anything can come up or out. And that is why it is an intensely physical and intimate journey with yourself when you work on the matter of fascia. Does that answer a bit your question?

QUESTION FROM THE AUDIENCE: I was curious whether you are exposed to scientific literature, and if this is important for your work. Upon which physiological knowledge is your work grounded, and what kind of knowledge do you use, based on what we know today about bodily, mental and affective states of being in the body with the body? That is big question. I was wondering which direction you would go through, or primarily, or what do you choose as your path.

MARGRÉT SARA GUÐJÓNSDÓTTIR: My main focus is on the »Perceptive Pedagogy« branch of the Danis Bois fascia therapy method. Dani Bois is a French osteopath who made many discoveries in the field of the connective tissue over the last 30 years. I have been studying his method and am also a manual therapist in the method by now. This knowledge is incredibly useful for my work with the dancers. It is about supporting people to move forwards; away from their former biographies and into the present. The work is conducted through the subjective and sensorial experience of the body. It is amazing to have that kind of knowledge while working with dancers and to be on this kind of artistic journey together, as well as to know how to be with people in the best way possible in these intensive situations that we have passed through in the work. Personally, I study manual therapy, meditation methods and the science of the subtle body so that I can get in touch with and discover the real meaning of cognitive plasticity, with a focus on deconditioning and listening to a person's biography.

QUESTION FROM THE AUDIENCE: I saw your performance *Conspiracy Ceremony – HYPERSONIC STATES* in November 2017 at the Sophiensaele in Berlin and was very impressed. I was really impressed by these energies around the dancers and the resonance that I could experience between myself as audience member and the dancer. I could see that there is a kind of relation between the dancers on the stage. My question is: how can this state become a choreography and how – if – you train this resonance between a dancer and yourself as a choreographer too?

MARGRÉT SARA GUÐJÓNSDÓTTIR: We emphasize the distinctive reality of connective tissue dialogue that exists between us as human beings, which can be palpably felt when we remain in a clear and aware resonance with it. It requires a lot of training and meditation and intimacy with your own tissues to be able to do that: that is the expertise I am training with the dancers through the *Full Drop Into The Body* practice. I have been practicing, processing and exploring the practice through my own body all these years, alongside the dancers of course, and before starting to work with others on it as well, as you know. I am one of the practitioners. One major goal that I set for myself when I started this journey as the choreographer was the desire to work with bodies like these and topics like these: diving into them to then reflect outwards the inner realities of the social political body of our times, as well as the ancient knowledge that we also carry from generation to generation within our bodies.

It is not a re-enactment or representation. Indeed, it is not a representation or a presentation. Rather it is a fully lived physical state and a tuning into rhythms of inner autonomous systems, which produces certain types of movements, imagery, presence, vibrations and a certain type of sensorial flavor for the audiences and the dancers. These particular states that we worked with came up during the working process and research (and we discarded many, many others that emerged but did not fit the topic of the performance). I tried to crack them open and ask: what is it that makes them resonate so strongly with the artistic theme? And how does the dancer relate to them? How can you talk about them together, in order to try to examine them more thoroughly? Can the dancers reproduce them on demand? And then how? Etcetera. In that sense, it is a very acrobatic and complex process. For instance, I could never have done the last piece we made if I would not have had two years of time and incredibly dedicated people.

Working Processes in Dance
The Poetics of a Morphing Body

Kat Válastur

In this chapter, I will discuss both my work and my working processes, particular in terms of one question that has become increasing prominent over time: What kind of bodies are we becoming in a radically transforming and ever more complex world?

In 2008 I made a piece in which I addressed the question: *what is left to be danced?* This inquiry threw me – literally and physically – to the floor, in the sense of questioning urgently the possibilities of answering: how *do* and even *can* we reply to this question? For me, a dance piece is usually the way to accomplish this task. When I followed this question it began to specifically address the aspect of time, as well as questions around *why do I dance?* Why do I want to dance, and what is there left to be danced for me? This was especially relevant considering the fact that there are so many things that have been danced. After ten years, this question has transformed into: *what kind of bodies are we becoming?* This also returns to the first question – *what is left to be danced?* – considering that, even if we become more complex, there will always be something that we have forgotten to dance.

I also need to ask: Why am I still choosing choreography as my method of making art? I persist in working with the body as a force, and consider the performing body to be in an extremely exposed transitional state, and therefore call it the »heroic body«. However, I do not only wish to depict its vulnerability, but even more so its exposure to the force fields of art, ecology, and technology, in relation to the primal springs of existence. The task that I must fulfill, using the process of choreography, arises directly from these considerations.

That is why the choreography itself must maintain a constant process of revealing the »heroic body«. Yet on the other hand the »heroic body« itself offers further possibilities upon which choreography can construct a unique language. In the body these possibilities are material: the skeleton, muscles, and figure all react to our contemporary condition, leading to a body marked by an internal personal rhythm. My goal is to give these tendencies the human grace that they are characterized by, that is to say: to offer space for the audience to reorganize its own emotional capacities.

I usually work with cycles of works, and in 2014 I began one called *The Marginal Sculptures of Newtopia*. What I usually do in my works is throw bodies into extreme conditions, or establish conditions that I want to develop and explore myself, via the body.

In 2014 I created the piece *GLAND*, in which the body appears to be in a condition of changing gravity. This was performed in a special room that I constructed with two walls and a floor shaped like a corner. I worked with perception by establishing a condition in which each surface could act as the reflection of the other. I moved as if gravity was changing the angle of its vector. It therefore looked as if I could walk on the floor, for the floor is the wall and the wall is the floor. In order to accomplish this, I had to place myself in a very particular position.

Figure 1: *GLAND* (2014). Choreographed and performed by Kat Válastur.

In this working process, I mostly laid sideways on the floor trying to produce a certain perspective/image for the audience, so that it would seem like I was actually standing on one of the walls, which was acting as the floor. In fact, the starting point of *GLAND* was not the movement, but actually a series of short science fiction stories that I wrote about the journey of a body in a fictional landscape. I tried to activate this landscape by experiencing the studio as a moving space of shifting gravity.

Immediately after but during the same year as *GLAND*, I made a group piece called *Ah! Oh! A Contemporary Ritual*. Here I also worked with a fictional condition, pretending that bodies had mutated from exposure to a certain outside influence. This imaginary process strongly affected the idea of what I am about to become/perform. *Ah! Oh! A Contemporary Ritual* contained several very important aspects concerning this process.[1] In *Ah! Oh! A Contemporary Ritual* I wanted to create a piece in which culture has collapsed and nothing remains but ruins. The world has somehow been destroyed in this post-apocalyptic scenario, and the survivors of this catastrophe enter a space and have to perform a ritual. It presumes that everything we have known about our society no longer exists. To respond to this condition, I told my dancers a very simple story: »There will be a group of people who will go to a forest. How will they begin again? How will they rebuild a cultural space?«

The archaic space of a circle came to my mind, in terms of a circle dance as the basis of forming a society. This is not unheard of, for circle dances are very common form in Greek folk culture for example. My main concern was in finding ways to break the banality of the circle dance without betraying its importance. Then I started to think of the type of bodies that I sought to explore: what are these beings? How do these people relate to each other? I imagined faces with blown cheeks, because they are holding air in their mouths. They also transmit an invisible force between themselves, and their hands are hidden in their pockets. Within this set of conditions, the question emerged: *what does it mean for these people to gather and allow themselves to be together?* There were also many questions regarding the aspect of the blown cheeks and what that might mean.

---

1 I refer to this work because I will later discuss *Rasp Your Soul*, to which it has a connection in terms of space, data and the skin, which I will mention later.

Figure 2: *Ah! Oh! A Contemporary Ritual* (2014). Choreographed by Kat Válastur.

I use references, but I consider them to resemble a memory. This is like when you read things or you interact with the world, and the vague reference of something or to something appears like a memory. Similarly, the blown cheeks appear because they contain data: they are bodies who have been exposed to too much input, which they cannot swallow, so it simply remains.

There is a moment in the piece in which one of the performers accelerates and, as if charged with an explosive force, breaks the circle. This explosion throws the other bodies into the space and transforms it into a techno-club. The space becomes a cultural memory and the bodies dancing in the club are carriers of that momentum. The whole scene is performed in slow motion, using a cinematic time lapse.

In my working process I usually include stories and images, and I give my dancers and performers a story to reflect upon and work with. When I describe an explosion, dancers need to vividly imagine and embody it. At the same time, they must sustain a very particular condition: that of the blown cheeks, which they carry throughout the hour-long piece. Towards the end of the piece, when they remove their jackets, they are each in their own space. This signals: I do not want to touch the others. This is a circle dance which nonetheless contains a lot of confrontation between each dancer and the meaning and image of what a circle dance must be or is supposed to be. Each dancer is afraid of touching the others. After this process, the dancers arrive at the point where they get rid of their jackets, which are metaphors for the skin-culture that shapes them.

After that moment, the group arrives at another state. Whenever I try to set a position in my work, I also affirm that there is always a point of exit. We dance until we can take our skin off – which indicates create spacing for rethinking. These exits are usually brief and do not last, but are nonetheless where I wish to bring the bodies to. It represents an opening, which I would like people to reflect upon.

Figure 3: *Ah! Oh! A Contemporary Ritual* (2014). Choreographed by Kat Válastur.

A circle of white light hovers in mid-air above the stage and the dancers. This light moves in relation to the performers, and has its own circular movement. It might resemble the rotating cursor on my apple computer when the system freezes. Or it could represent the element of time or perhaps the eye of »Big Brother.« Either way, it is political because it extends beyond the movement itself. The movement does not cease along with what my body is doing, but rather relates to which space and condition I am entering. This is like a dangerous zone in which I as an individual am struggling to cope. My body must allow itself to lose control, but simultaneously not lose control and keep resisting, which is a complex situation for a body to be in.

Rasp Your Soul is a piece I did in 2017, and it belongs to a new cycle of works in which the body has »swallowed« a large amount of data. This data is somehow inside the body, while we ourselves are also the space of data. This piece represents a shift to a new kind of process. In the past I have worked from outside to inside: I set an environment with external conditions, and then placed the dancers inside a field to deal with that condition. However, this new piece used the opposite process. The body was carrying a condition, which in *Rasp Your Soul* was represented by the data, and the performer had to bring this out and make it visible.

QUESTION FROM THE AUDIENCE: Many choreographers currently work with opening the body and going over the borders of the body. There is also a transformation because of the digital information that is already in the body. The body is not identified as only organic, because technology is already being integrated in the body. What are your ideas about opening or closing the borders – how do you deal with these ideas?

KAT VÁLASTUR: This is exactly the subject that I am working on, in the sense of how many bodies we are. It is about the moment that everything started being more digital, and how we embody this change. This constant encounter affects us in a very real way. We still have the same bodies we had centuries ago, and our biology remains the same. My original body is old but then there is also a new body that I can perceive, and which has different possibilities, so it is complex.

The question of what is real versus what is fictional is one of consciousness, as well as the constant process of constructing consciousness and how it relates to the unconscious. I somehow encounter all of these ideas in the aspect of *Rasp Your Soul* that asks: where is the self in the bodies that we are today. It resides somewhere between all that we are and all that we consider ourselves to be, right? In the philosophical Deleuzian tradition I am a body, but this becomes more complex when what I consider my body to be also comes to include the body of my avatar. This led me to a new approach in the research process, in terms of applying the effect of morphing as a tool for inventing movement, and by using a liquefying process to create movement. This flowed from one becoming to the other; from one image to the other; from one gender to the other, and so on. During this process of discovering other bodies within our own, we replied on our imaginations extensively. It is not about acting a role, but rather is very much about developing a new language. You are a performer, while simultaneously also the creator of yourself, like being both a god and a demon.

Figure 4: *Rasp Your Soul* (2017). Choreographed by Kat Valástur, performed by Enrico Ticconi.

The piece is titled *Rasp Your Soul*, which itself is quite open to interpretation. Some people perceive it as negative, while others think it is positive, in the sense of asking: what is there? »To rasp« is an action: you can rasp a piece of marble until it is perfectly shaped. This also relates to capitalism, as to rasp something is to make it look as shaped, sculpted and designed as possible, in order to be appealing. *Rasp Your Soul* is a solo work. I usually begin from elementary forms, such as a solo, but this was the first time that I did a solo work that I was not performing myself. I chose a very special performer for the piece, Enrico Ticconi, whom I have known since 2012. I particularly liked the idea of facing someone, rather than working alone.

In *Rasp Your Soul* I would call the performer a humanoid with a sensitive skin, and the piece explores the moment in which the performer's body is exposed to several inputs. If there is an outside trying to manipulate the body, there is an inside that responds back with its own inputs. Sometimes these inputs become mantras, thus creating absurd and uncanny momentums. The whole thing originated when I thought: »Silicon Valley is inside of us, we have ›swallowed‹ it, and we are living in this kind of reality and cannot step back.« While working on the piece, we started thinking a bit about very common things, such as avatars. I connected that idea to the world of video games, in which I (the player) am the avatar and at the same time I am not the avatar. Or rather I am in control of the avatar that I am. This creates a form of unconscious that is – I would say – as vivid as my unconscious and as mystical as my unconscious. What I think created this piece was the mystical relation that I have with something else who is not the other, but rather a form of *otherness*, and which is supposed to be me, or that is me but is simultaneously not exactly me.

The performer is a very elusive kind of being, in the sense that he both transforms and does not transform anything. One does not know what is coming from outside, or how this constant relation between control and freedom exists in a very dense relation. To intensify this whole process I relied upon the voice, which was a very important aspect, because the sounds that the performer creates are intricately related to the movement. The sound of the voice is elaborated by pitch shifts, which form high and low noises. The alienation and constant motion of the voice between different vocals manifests the elusiveness of gender, as well as indicating the transformation of the dancer into a digital entity or a wild animal. This body changes forms, even turning to a liquefied body, and therefore I also refer to it as a mythological being or a post-mythological being. Mythological time exists in this piece because, just as in a motion capture, one can become anything that moves and talks. It appears easy to become, say, a wolf.

So perhaps this more elusive and liquid form can create an exit, by which I mean a place of rethinking. We are constantly trapped in a consumer capitalist loop, but one must ask what the eventual position might be that could offer a kind of key to open the door. I always need to reflect upon this exit for myself, and I need to create this exit for myself. At the same time it is kind of hilarious, because we seem to be cartoon characters trapped in our own super-saturated life, and I also try to make this element visible in my work. I am interested in pointing out these comic and tragic aspects of our aspirations, so I use the language like a script that the performer articulates, as if it was data injected into the body.

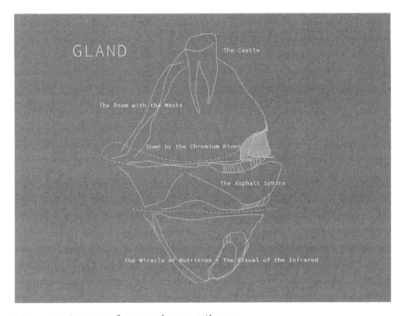

Figure 5: Diagram of *GLAND* by Kat Válastur.

As in *Ah! Oh!* and *GLAND*, I wrote six short science-fiction stories in order to place the body into different rooms. In *GLAND* the room has two vertical walls and a horizontal floor, and the body goes into these two dimensions. But for me the space that I was entering was much richer: more than just two walls and a floor. I therefore had to write stories that I could enter, so as to create a different reality in which I could perform. You could watch me move within this set-up, but I was actually performing a journey (to the spaces of the short-stories) that was hidden in my movements and gestures.

I made a special diagram-map to reflect this particular journey. Each space on the map reflected an event, and they included: the castle, a room with masks, a chromium river etc. For example, the room with masks brought together the painting of Picasso's »les demoiselles d'avignon« with a mutated gaze looking at all surfaces as if they were made of aluminum, and that gaze slowly transforms the painting's texture into that metal. I also created a mythological event out of the relation that we have with the material that laptops are made of, and then I embodied this in the tension between the primitive faces of Picasso and that aluminum sensation via the gaze, which became a kinetic monument in the performing space of *GLAND*. I also performed a series of masks by placing my hands on my face, slowly passing from one to another in fragments. The atoms of the aluminum are shaped in a face-centered cubic structure, and I brought the elements together by having my face changing inside the unique set of *GLAND*: the cut-in-half cubic room.

In *Rasp Your Soul*, I sought to include the voice and to think about space and time. Time is extremely fragmented in this piece, and the body can jump scenes like in the cinema, in an editing process that cut from one thing to another. Some words formed a script and appeared in the rehearsals, such as the term »disconnect« or the request »do not disconnect«. Because connecting and disconnecting are used freely and frequently in a digital sense, we worked on the question of how the performer can produce and show connectivity, as well as obeying the request to »not disconnect«, while questions of »from what« and »towards what« remained unanswered.

DISCUSSION with the Audience

QUESTION FROM THE AUDIENCE: I was wondering if you use the term »energy« in your choreographic thinking and, if so, how it relates to imaginations and the stories.

KAT VÁLASTUR: Energy as a force or...

QUESTION: The energy that circulates along the bodies. What circulates between the bodies in the group?

KAT VÁLASTUR: I call the space between the bodies »a field of forces«. This is an otherwise unnamed force that causes the body to react – the body alone has to deal with another force that affects it and makes it react, or does not. When there are other bodies involved, they have to deal with multiple forces. They are in a force that affects them, and it forms their movements as well as the way they relate to each other, which together creates another degree of scale for the forces between the bodies. My pieces are very energetic, and a certain kind of magnetic field is always constructed that makes things quite intense. We get to a point where things get warm: my pieces are warm pieces, and precisely crafted.

QUESTION: And you would also use the story and imagination to sculpt these relations or fields?

KAT VÁLASTUR: Yes: For example, in *Ah! Oh!* there is a downfall, which we must resist in order to avoid falling, and which thus must be embodied. Yet the aesthetic aspect is not enough – the dancers have to move beyond that. It is important for each performer to really understand how they charge themselves with the image of the downfall.

QUESTION: Do you also use a certain body work, such as techniques that are more physical, after beginning with words and language?

KAT VÁLASTUR: Language is always present – especially when describing and articulating a space or state that the body should enter. In the piece *CORPUS III* the body was fragmented because time was fragmented. This represented a very specific condition, wherein the body entered a time field and a time lapse, and I had to find a method of kinetically embodying this. The piece was divided into chapters like a book, and in each the body had to enter a different narrative: this is how we created a method of working with the body. There is no story here in the sense of a beginning, middle and an end, rather it is more like parts coming together. I provide a lot of the movement myself by going to the studio three months prior, researching until I discover the core of the piece, and then only after that do I invite people to join me.

QUESTION: I just wanted to come back to a sentence you used in the beginning: that you are interested in putting bodies into a certain condition. I think this is interesting. Could you tell us what condition you were interested in *Rasp Your Soul?*

KAT VÁLASTUR: This condition is complex, and it originated from the permeability of the skin. This was more complicated than in *GLAND*, where there were gravitational shifts, or in *Ah! Oh!* when there was a circle dance. In *Rasp Your Soul* this was deeper, and came from questioning: what comes through my skin, and how does it affects me? This was about how inputs affect me, which maybe I still do not fully understand. It was also about something unconscious, and how to construct it using choreography and then perform it on stage.

QUESTION: I was wondering how much did you choreograph the movement (the dancer's movement) and how much came from him? How did you work with him?

KAT VÁLASTUR: I choreograph everything, but we worked a lot on the morphing in order to try to find a particular type of quality. How do you transition from one movement or sign into another, whether it be a sign or persona or identity? This process is very difficult when one is constantly exposed to these different layers and qualities and inputs. The task is to capture and embody them, but at the same time the morphing occurs rapidly, so the dancer has to slide fluidly from one image to the next. We did the necessary research together, and worked together one on one. He could propose five movements, oriented around a sign that meant something and communicated something, and then we created variations based around that – it was a lot to coordinate.

QUESTION: How do you develop the tasks for the performers?
KAT VÁLASTUR: I will give an example: in *Rasp Your Soul* the imperative »do not disconnect« raises the question: Do not disconnect with me? With what? How do we relate to technological aspects, or to networking? I wanted to find a force in that sense. There are all these inputs and features, but there is also a body that accepts and resists. These bodies contain something mythological, which is not necessarily a reference to mythology, but rather it is about constructing something fictional that says something about the ways we have created our world.

QUESTION: It would be interesting to also reflect on the finished work, despite the importance of the working process, since it seems to me that there is a strong narrative line and a strong narrative aspect to it. How is this connected to the states and the relation to force?
KAT VÁLASTUR: Apart from the required movement, I think this is the way we talk in the choreographic process. These forces are part of life, and discussing the work makes certain aspects very real. I will bring a word or an image or some information from a real-life example, and then we will go beyond it. We will create a movement and then a fictional condition, and then we will move through that strata that evolves with it, and the layers of the elements that are constructing it. It all comes together and becomes processed, like a chemical process.

QUESTION: Do you think about where you would like to direct your audience's thoughts? Perceptions?

KAT VÁLASTUR: I believe that, in general, there is no communication in art, and there is nothing to understand. People will experience something and then will perhaps think something about it. However, I perceive art to be a very closed system. As viewers, we perceive in relation to who we are and how we think. I cannot influence what others think, so instead I only try to be true to myself. I would really like it if people were moved after seeing one of my works, but I do not expect them to understand my intentions.

QUESTION: *Rasp Your Soul* is the beginning of a new trilogy? Where do you want to go after, and what questions are arising from the work now?
KAT VÁLASTUR: The cycle is called *The Staggered Dances of Beauty*. These works address the ontological question of what kind of bodies are we becoming. I want to continue working with the complexity of our bodies: that is the discourse, but I am heading towards a poetic and a rather absurd result rather than something didactic.

Notes on Contributors

Susan Leigh Foster, choreographer and scholar, is Distinguished Professor in the Department of World Arts and Cultures/Dance at UCLA. She is author of *Reading Dancing* (University of California Press 1986), *Choreographing Narrative* (Indiana University Press 1996), *Dances that Describe Themselves* (Wesleyan University Press 2002), *Choreographing Empathy* (Routledge 2011) and, most recently, *Valuing Dance: Commodities and Gifts in Motion* (Oxford University Press 2019). Three of her danced lectures can be found at the Pew Center for Arts and Heritage website: http://danceworkbook.pcah.us/susan-foster/index.html.

Barbara Gronau is Professor for Theatre Studies at the Berlin University of Arts and Speaker of the Research Training Group »Knowledge in the Arts«, funded by the German Research Fund (DFG). She received her Ph.D. for her dissertation *Theaterinstallationen. Performative Räume bei Beuys, Boltanski und Kabakov* (Wilhelm Fink Verlag 2010), for which Gronau obtained the »Joseph Beuys Award for Research«. Since her interest is also in theatre practice, Gronau worked as a dramaturg and curator for several theatre productions and festivals. Her publications include: *HOW TO FRAME. On the Threshold of Performance and Visual Arts* (Sternberg Press 2016), *Aesthetics of Standstill*, co-ed. R. Goerling, L. Schwarte (Sternberg Press 2019).

Margrét Sara Guðjónsdóttir is an Icelandic choreographer living and working in Berlin. Since 2010 she has toured internationally her seven full length peformances and four comissioned full length works, two of which were created for the *Swedish Cullberg Ballet* (2014/2017). Her performance works – *Pervasive Magnetic Stimuli* (2018), *Conspiracy Ceremony - HYPERSONIC STATES* (2017), *In The Blind Spot* (2015), *Blind Spotting* (2014) and *SPOTTED* (2014) – have been shown and premiered in Berlin at *Sophiensaele*. Margrét has developed a new genre of performative body language, and an original working method that directly informs her creative outcomes. Her work keeps on taking shape from the ongoing in-depth research that accesses physiological and emotional sub-worlds. Displaying the politics of intimacy is a core theme within her choreographic work while working with and exploring pathologies of the social political body within our own bodies. In 2017 she started her ongoing collaboration on Somatic Archiving with Professor Susan Kozel, Malmö University.

Maximilian Haas (Dr.) is a performance and media theorist and a drama-turge, based in Berlin. He is a postdoc researcher at the DFG Research Train-ing Group »Knowledge in the Arts« at the Berlin University of Arts. Haas studied at the Institute for Applied Theatre Studies in Giessen. His practice based PhD project *Animals on Stage. An Aesthetic Ecology of Performance* (Kad-mos 2018) was affiliated with the Academy of Media Arts Cologne (KHM). Recent academic lectures and articles have been centred around the aesthet-ics of dance, performance, and artistic research, as well as issues of science and technology studies, and the philosophy of post-structuralism, new ma-terialism, and pragmatism.

Sabine Huschka (PD Dr.) is a dance and theatre scholar, based in Berlin. Since 2015 she has been head of the DFG research project ›Transgressions‹ at the Inter-University Centre for Dance Berlin (HZT) and guest scholar at the Research Training Group »Knowledge in the Arts« at the Berlin Univer-sity of Arts. She received her PhD at Humboldt University Berlin with the study *Merce Cunningham und der Moderne Tanz* (Königshausen & Neumann 1998) and her habilitation at University of Leipzig (2011) with her studies on *Wissenskultur Tanz: Der choreografierte Körper im Theater*. Her publications include: *Moderner Tanz. Konzepte – Stile – Utopien* (rowohlts enzyclopädie 2002/2012) and *Tanz/Wissen. Choreographierte Körper im theatron. Auftritte und Theorie ästhetischen Wissens.* (epodium 2019).

Susanne Franco is Assistant Professor at Ca' Foscari University of Venice. Her research interests and publications focus on modern and contemporary dance, and dance research methodology. She has authored *Martha Graham* (L'Epos 2003) and *Frédéric Flamand* (L'Epos 2004), and edited the special issue *Ausdruckstanz: il corpo, la danza e la critica*, in *Biblioteca Teatrale* (2006).

With Marina Nordera she edited *Dance Discourses. Keywords in Dance Research* (Routledge 2007), and *Ricordanze. Memoria in movimento e coreografie della storia* (UTET Università 2010). As curator she collaborates with the Fondazione Querini Stampalia (Venice), the Foundation Pinault (Venice), and together with Roberto Casarotto has curated dance events for the Hangar Bicocca (Milan). She is responsible for the Ca' Foscari uniti for project *DANCING MUSEUMS. The Democracy of Beings* (Creative Europe 2018-2021).

Susan Kozel is a Professor at the School of Arts and Communication at Malmö University in Sweden. She works at the convergence between performance, philosophy and responsive digital technologies. Previous publications include *Closer: Performance, Technologies, Phenomenology* (MIT Press 2007), plus many shorter articles and essays that can be found on www.su sankozel.com. Alongside her academic writing, she collaborates on artistic productions (recently with Margrét Sara Guðjónsdóttir and Gibson/Martelli) and has an archive of performative lectures on philosophical and artistic topics. Current research takes a political turn towards *Affective Choreographies and Performances of Encryption*.

Meghan Quinlan is a US-based dance scholar researching the circulation and politics of Gaga, the improvisatory dance language developed by Israeli choreographer Ohad Naharin. She earned her PhD in Critical Dance Studies from the University of California, Riverside and has since taught at universities in California and Georgia. Her work has been published in journals such as *Dance Research Journal* and *TDR: The Drama Review*.

Lucia Ruprecht is a Fellow of Emmanuel College and an affiliated Lecturer at the Section of German and Dutch, University of Cambridge, UK. She has published widely on dance, literature, and film. She is author of *Dances of the Self in Heinrich von Kleist, E.T.A. Hoffmann and Heinrich Heine* (Ashgate 2006), and of *Gestural Imaginaries: Dance and Cultural Theory in the Early Twentieth Century* (Oxford University Press 2019), has edited a special section of the online journal *Performance Philosophy*, entitled *Towards an Ethics of Gesture* (2017), and co-edited *Performance and Performativity in German Cultural Studies* (Peter Lang 2003), and *New German Dance Studies* (University of Illinois Press 2012), and a special issue of *German Life & Letters*, entitled *Cultural Pleasure* (2009).

Gerald Siegmund is Professor of Applied Theatre Studies at the Justus-Liebig University in Giessen, Germany. He studied Theatre, English and French literature at Goethe-University in Frankfurt a.M.. Until 2008 he was assistant professor at the Institute of Theatre Studies in Bern, Switzerland. Among his research interests are theatre and memory, aesthetics, dance, performance and theatre since the beginning of the 20th century. He was head of the DFG-research group »Theatre as Dispositif« where he researched the theatrical dispositifs in Germany since the 1960s. Between 2012 and 2016 Gerald Siegmund was president of the German Association for Theatre Studies (GTW). His most recent publications are *Jérôme Bel. Dance, Theatre, and the Subject* (Palgrave Macmillan 2017) and together with Rebekah Kowal und Randy Martin *The Oxford Handbook of Dance and Politics* (Oxford University Press 2017).

Christina Thurner is Professor for Dance Studies at the Institute of Theatre Studies, University of Bern/Switzerland. She was a Research Assistant in the German Literature seminar at the University of Basel from 1996 to 2007. She was awarded her doctorate in 2001 and her habilitation in 2008 with the study *Beredte Körper – bewegte Seelen. Zum Diskurs der doppelten Bewegung in Tanztexten* (transcript 2009). Main areas of research include history, discourses and aesthetics of dance from the 18th century until today, contemporary dance and performance, historiography, dance criticism, autobiographical studies.

Kat Válastur is claimed as one of the most exciting choreographers in the Berlin dance scene. Her works are defined by the creation of a distinctive dance language. Through her groundbreaking works notions of fragmented narratives, time lapses and virtuality emerge. Highly intense atmospheres are created, challenging the senses and the rules of ordinary perception. In 2017 after her retrospective »We were better in the future« at HAU Hebbel am Ufer, she started working on a new circle of works with the title »The staggered dances of beauty«. The first work of the circle *Rasp Your Soul* premiered on the 2nd of November 2017 at HAU Hebbel am Ufer. Kat Válastur's work is presented internationally.

List of Figures

Lucia Ruprecht

p. 127, Figure 1: *The Pictures Generation, 1974-1984*, The Metropolitan Museum of Art, The Henry R. Kravis Wing, The Tisch Galleries, April 21 – August 2, 2009. View of three images by Robert Longo displayed in the entry hall of the Metropolitan Museum. New York, Metropolitan Museum of Art. © 2018. Image copyright The Metropolitan Museum of Art/Art Resource/ Scala, Florence.

p. 129, Figure 2: Boris Charmatz, *10000 Gestures*, Mayfield Depot, Manchester, 10 July 2017, Photographed by Tristram Kenton © Tristram Kenton.

Margrét Sara Guðjónsdóttir, Susan Kozel

p. 181, Figure 1: *Pervasive Magnetic Stimuli.* Choreographed by Margrét Sara Guðjónsdóttir, Sophiensaele Berlin 2018. Photographed by Eva Schmid-huber.

Kat Válastur

p. 194, Figure 1: *GLAND.* Choreographed and performed by Kat Válastur. Photographed by Dorothea Tuch, 2014.

p. 196, Figure 2: *Ah!Oh! A Contemporary Ritual.* Choreographed by Kat Válastur. Photographed by Dorothea Tuch, 2014.

p. 197, Figure 3: *Ah!Oh! A Contemporary Ritual.* Choreographed by Kat Válastur. Photographed by Dorothea Tuch, 2014.

p. 199, Figure 4: *Rasp Your Soul.* Choreographed by Kat Válastur, performed by Enrico Ticconi. Photographed by Dorothea Tuch, 2017.

p. 201, Figure 5: Diagram of *GLAND* by Kat Válastur. © Kat Válastur.